Flexibility Fuels PersonalProgress

Flexibility Fuels PersonalProgress

Rafeal Mechlore

UNIEK ENTERPRISES

CONTENTS

8.2 Embracing Failure for Growth

INTRODUCTION

In a world set apart by fast change, vulnerability, and ceaseless development, the capacity to adjust and flex is presently not a simple resource — it's a goal. The time we end up in requests a degree of flexibility that outperforms what past ages experienced. Our lives are formed by a many-sided interaction of mechanical headways, moving financial scenes, and exceptional worldwide difficulties. To flourish in this unique climate, to graph our course in a universe of consistent movement, adaptability turns into the essential fuel for individual advancement.

The excursion toward individual advancement is a significant and profoundly individual mission. It's the quest for development, satisfaction, and self-acknowledgment. It envelops our expert goals, the connections we assemble, our wellbeing and prosperity, and our general feeling of direction. However, the way to advance is frequently loaded with deterrents, turns, and unexpected diversions. To explore this complicated landscape really, we want the ability to adjust, to twist without breaking, and to track down strength in our adaptability.

This book, "Adaptability Energizes Individual Advancement," sets out on a journey into the core of versatility. An excursion investigates the science, brain research, and reasonableness of being adaptable in a steadily impacting world. Through its pages, we will uncover the significant effect that versatility has on our self-improvement, our professions, our connections, and our prosperity.

The Test of Progress

Change is the steady friend of the human experience. From the earliest days of our reality, we've confronted the tenacious recurring pattern of seasons, the change of social orders, and the rise of new advancements. Change has forever been the setting of our lives, yet what recognizes our ongoing time is the speed and size of progress.

In the range of only years and years, we've seen the approach of the web, the expansion of cell phones, the globalization of business sectors, and the ascent of man-made reasoning. These seismic movements have introduced a time of remarkable interconnectedness and data sharing, in a general sense modifying the manner in which we work, impart, and see our general surroundings.

While these headways bring striking open doors, they additionally present one of a kind difficulties. The very advances that guarantee to upgrade our lives can leave us feeling

overpowered, separated, and unsure. The conventional profession ways that once given a feeling of dependability and security are currently portrayed by instability and unconventionality. Furthermore, the speed of progress can leave us longing briefly of break, a position of sureness in a world that feels progressively liquid.

The Call for Adaptability

It is exactly at this time of transition that the call for adaptability resonates with lucidity and desperation. Adaptability isn't just a response to transform; it's a pro-active position towards life. It's the acknowledgment that the world will proceed to advance, and our ability to flourish relies upon our eagerness to develop with it.

Adaptability isn't tied in with giving up our qualities or standards. Rather, it's tied in with having the flexibility to maintain these qualities while exploring the steadily moving scenes of our lives. It's the capacity to survey, turn, and recalibrate our course when important, all while remaining consistent with our center convictions and goals.

Consider the bamboo tree, which twists effortlessly even with wild breezes. It influences and adjusts to the evolving powers, never snapping or breaking. This surprising versatility is a demonstration of the force of adaptability. In our own lives, we also can develop this capacity to twist, to change, and to persevere through life's tempests.

The Commitment of Individual Advancement

As we leave on this investigation of adaptability and its part in private advancement, it's essential to explain what we mean by "individual advancement." While the definition fluctuates from one individual to another, it frequently envelops a few key aspects:

Proficient Development: This incorporates progressing in one's profession, improving abilities, and accomplishing objectives that lead to monetary soundness and occupation fulfillment.

Connections: Building and sustaining significant associations with others, cultivating solid and strong associations with family, companions, and partners.

Prosperity: Dealing with one's physical and emotional wellness, overseeing pressure, and tracking down equilibrium and satisfaction throughout everyday life.

Self-satisfaction: Seeking after one's interests, side interests, and individual objectives, and discovering a feeling of direction and satisfaction in those undertakings.

Versatility: Fostering the ability to return from mishaps, gain from disappointments, and persist notwithstanding misfortune.

Flexibility: Embracing change, being available to new encounters, and having the right stuff to change and flourish in unique conditions.

In every one of these aspects, adaptability assumes a crucial part. The ongoing idea empowers us to explore the difficulties and vulnerabilities that definitely emerge in our quest for progress. It engages us to turn when our underlying plans turn out badly, to gain from our errors, and to persistently refine our way ahead.

A Guide for the Excursion

As we dig further into the domain of adaptability and its significant effect on private advancement, this book will be your aide and sidekick. Across its sections, we will investigate the science behind flexibility, the brain research that supports it, and the useful techniques to upgrade it. We will find how adaptability applies to each element of individual advancement, from profession and connections to wellbeing and self-satisfaction.

You'll find accounts of people who have saddled the force of adaptability to beatoverwhelming difficulties and make amazing progress. We will dive into the apparatuses and methods that can assist you with developing adaptability in your own life. What's more, in particular, we will leave on an excursion of self-revelation, perceiving that the way to individual advancement isn't an objective yet a consistent development.

It is our expectation that this book will act as a wellspring of motivation and direction, empowering you to embrace adaptability as a power for individual change. Together, we will open the potential inside you to endure the hardships of progress as well as to tackle their energy to move you toward your goals.

The world might be in a condition of steady motion, yet inside you lies the ability to adjust, develop, and flourish. With adaptability as your fuel, individual advancement becomes a chance as well as a reality ready to be understood. Thus, let us set out on this excursion together, as we investigate how adaptability powers individual advancement and enables us to explore the consistently changing scene of life.

1 |

Chapter 1

Defining Flexibility And Personal Progress

During a time set apart by tireless change and flightiness, the ideas of adaptability and individual advancement have become the overwhelming focus. As the world develops at an uncommon speed, people are constrained to adjust, learn, and develop to stay up with the moving scene. In this investigation, we will dive into the major meanings of adaptability and individual advancement, looking at how these two ideas converge and entwine to profoundly mold our lives.

Figuring out Adaptability

The Embodiment of Adaptability

Adaptability, in its embodiment, is the capacity to twist without breaking, to adjust to new conditions, and to embrace change with versatility and elegance. It is the ability to answer life's difficulties and valuable open doors with a receptive outlook and an eagerness to change. Adaptability permits us to explore the intricacies of a powerful world, and it reaches out a long ways past the actual domain.

The Multidimensionality of Adaptability

Actual Adaptability: The capacity of the body to stretch, curve, and move easily. Actual adaptability is significant for keeping up with in general wellbeing and prosperity.

Mental Adaptability: The ability to adjust one's contemplations and mental cycles in light of new data or evolving conditions. It includes receptiveness, innovativeness, and the capacity to think about elective viewpoints.

Profound Adaptability: The ability of overseeing and directing one's feelings in various circumstances. Close to home adaptability empowers us to answer adaptively to testing profound encounters.

Relational Adaptability: The capacity to explore and acclimate to social elements, impart successfully, and assemble and keep up with solid connections.

Vocation Adaptability: The ability to adjust to changing workplaces, secure new abilities, and seek after open doors for proficient development and advancement.

Way of life Adaptability: The readiness to change one's schedules, propensities, and needs in arrangement with developing life conditions and individual objectives.

The Job of Adaptability in Self-awareness

Adaptability isn't only a receptive quality; it is a proactive power for self-awareness. It engages us to embrace change as a chance for improvement instead of a wellspring of dread or obstruction. As we develop adaptability in different components of our lives, we become stronger, versatile, and fit for exploring the intricacies of the advanced world.

The Quest for Individual Advancement

Characterizing Individual Advancement

Proficient Progression: Progressing in one's vocation, accomplishing profession objectives, and consistently gaining new abilities and information.

Connections and Social Associations: Building and sustaining significant connections, encouraging sound social associations, and developing compassion and understanding.

Physical and Mental Prosperity: Dealing with one's actual well-being through exercise, nourishment, and taking care of oneself, as well as keeping up with emotional wellness through pressure the executives and mindfulness.

Self-satisfaction and Reason: Seeking after interests, leisure activities, and individual interests that give pleasure and satisfaction, and adjusting one's life to a feeling of direction and importance.

Versatility and Flexibility: Fostering the ability to return from difficulties, gain from disappointments, and adjust to evolving conditions.

The Significance of Individual Advancement

Individual advancement isn't just an issue of individual satisfaction yet additionally a critical driver of cultural headway. As people endeavor to develop and create, they add to the aggregate advancement of networks and social orders. Besides, individual advancement frequently prompts expanded prosperity, fulfillment, and a more prominent feeling of direction throughout everyday life.

The Association Among Adaptability and Individual Advancement

Adaptability and individual advancement are inherently associated. Adaptability is the instrument that empowers us to explore the difficulties and open doors that emerge on the way of individual advancement. Without adaptability, we risk becoming unbending, impervious to change, and unfit to adjust to developing conditions.

The Crossing point of Adaptability and Individual Advancement

Adjusting to Accomplish Progress

Profession Development: In a quickly changing position market, vocation adaptability is fundamental. People who are available to securing new abilities and adjusting to advancing jobs are bound to accomplish proficient advancement.

Connections: Relational adaptability assumes an essential part in building and keeping up with sound connections. The capacity to impart, split the difference, and adjust to the changing elements of connections is vital to individual advancement in this area.

Prosperity: Profound and mental adaptability are vital to overseeing pressure, adapting to difficulties, and keeping up with mental and close to home prosperity. An adaptable way to deal with taking care of oneself and wellbeing upholds individual advancement in this aspect.

Self-satisfaction: Chasing after private interests and interests requires adaptability concerning using time productively and needs. A versatile way of life that obliges self-satisfaction attempts adds to individual advancement.

Versatility and Variation: The strength acquired through adaptability empowers people to return quickly from misfortunes, gain from disappointments, and proceed with their excursion of individual advancement.

Way of life Decisions: Adaptability in way of life decisions, like sustenance and exercise, permits people to change their propensities and schedules to line up with their developing wellbeing and prosperity objectives.

The Collaboration of Adaptability and Individual Advancement
Adaptability and individual advancement are not restricting powers; they are synergistic. Adaptability engages people to explore change and vulnerability, empowering them to gain ground in different components of their lives. Thusly, individual advancement cultivates a feeling of achievement and satisfaction that supports one's flexibility and strength.

The Advantages of Adaptability for Individual Advancement
Upgrading Strength
One of the essential advantages of adaptability chasing after private advancement is its ability to upgrade versatility. Flexibility is the capacity to endure misfortune, recuperate from mishaps, and adjust to evolving conditions. Adaptability furnishes people with the apparatuses to stand up to difficulties with flexibility and return from disappointments with reestablished assurance.

Empowering Variation

Transformation is the foundation of individual advancement. Without the capacity to adjust, people risk stagnation and botched open doors for development. Adaptability works with transformation by empowering people to evaluate and change their techniques, objectives, and activities in light of evolving conditions.

Advancing Learning and Development

An adaptable mentality advances constant learning and development. At the point when people are available to new encounters and viewpoints, they are bound to obtain new abilities, extend their insight, and expand their perspectives. This obligation to deep rooted learning is fundamental for individual advancement.

Fortifying Connections

Relational adaptability is pivotal for building and keeping up with solid connections. It includes undivided attention, sympathy, viable correspondence, and the capacity to productively determine clashes. Solid, adaptable connections offer close to home help and add to in general prosperity, cultivating individual advancement.

Encouraging Advancement and Imagination

Mental adaptability fills advancement and inventiveness. At the point when people can adjust their reasoning and investigate various methodologies, they are bound to produce imaginative thoughts and arrangements. This imaginative flexibility can prompt advancement in different parts of life, including vocation and self-satisfaction.

Improving Profound Prosperity

Close to home adaptability adds to profound prosperity by empowering people to successfully deal with their feelings. It includes perceiving and managing feelings, adjusting profound reactions to various circumstances, and keeping up with close to home equilibrium. Close to home prosperity is an essential part of individual advancement.

The Difficulties of Adaptability in Private Advancement
Protection from Change

While adaptability is an important resource, it tends to be trying for people who oppose change. Certain individuals find solace in everyday practice and commonality, making it hard for them to embrace new open doors or change their objectives. Beating protection from change is a basic move toward tackling adaptability for individual advancement.

Feeling of dread toward Vulnerability

Vulnerability frequently goes with change, and as far as some might be concerned, it tends to be a wellspring of uneasiness. The feeling of dread toward the obscure can ruin people from facing challenges or chasing after new ways, in any event, when those ways hold the potential for individual advancement. Figuring out how to oversee and explore vulnerability is fundamental.

Adjusting Transformation and Steadiness

Adaptability doesn't suggest consistent change; it includes finding some kind of harmony among transformation and soundness. A few people might battle with tracking down this equilibrium, swaying between an excess of progress and a lot of unbending nature. Accomplishing harmony is a test yet a fundamental one for individual advancement.

Defeating Misfortunes and Disappointments

Adaptability prepares people to return quickly from difficulties and disappointments, however it doesn't take out the profound cost that these encounters can have. The test lies in keeping up with inspiration and assurance notwithstanding affliction, involving difficulties as venturing stones as opposed to hindrances.

Relational Difficulties

Relational adaptability can be especially difficult while managing clashes or troublesome connections. Figuring out how to adjust correspondence styles, explore clashes, and put down stopping points while keeping up with sound connections requires ability and practice.

Developing Adaptability for Individual Advancement

Developing Actual Adaptability

Exercise and Extending: Integrating standard active work and extending practices into your normal improves actual adaptability, adding to generally speaking prosperity.

Yoga and Pilates: Practices like yoga and Pilates are explicitly intended to work on actual adaptability, equilibrium, and strength.

Developing Mental Adaptability

Reflection and Care: These practices advance liberality and mental adaptability by empowering present-second mindfulness and non-critical reasoning.

Imaginative Pursuits: Participating in inventive exercises, like composition, workmanship, or music, empowers unique reasoning and the investigation of novel thoughts.

Developing Close to home Adaptability

Feeling Guideline: Foster techniques for perceiving and controlling feelings, for example, journaling, profound breathing, and care.

Sympathy: Practice compassion by effectively paying attention to other people and attempting to grasp their points of view and feelings.

Developing Relational Adaptability

Successful Correspondence: Further develop relational abilities by looking for criticism, rehearsing undivided attention, and learning compromise strategies.

Limit Setting: Foster the capacity to define and keep up with solid limits in connections to guarantee common regard and prosperity.

Developing Vocation Adaptability

Deep rooted Learning: Embrace nonstop advancing by signing up for courses, going to studios, and looking for chances to secure new abilities.

Organizing: Construct an expert organization to remain informed about industry drifts and set out open doors for professional success.

Developing Way of life Adaptability

Objective Setting: Set adaptable, versatile objectives that consider change as conditions change.

Using time effectively: Foster powerful time usage techniques to oblige different needs and responsibilities.

The Job of Adaptability in Beating Difficulties

Building Flexibility

Strength is the capacity to quickly return from misfortune, and adaptability is a center part of flexibility. At the point when people face difficulties, their versatility and eagerness to change their methodologies empower them to continue on and recuperate from misfortunes.

Embracing Disappointment as a Learning An open door

Adaptability urges people to see disappointment not as a loss but rather as an important learning an open door. By adjusting their methodology and gaining from botches, people can transform difficulties into venturing stones on their way to individual advancement.

Flourishing in Unsure Times

In a time described by vulnerability, adaptability is a significant resource. It empowers people to explore eccentric circumstances, go with informed choices, and change their arrangements as conditions advance. Flourishing in dubious times requires an adaptable mentality and a receptiveness to change.

Overseeing Pressure and Conquering Difficulty

Adaptability in adapting to pressure is fundamental for keeping up with mental and profound prosperity. People who can adjust their pressure the board systems to suit various circumstances are better prepared to defeat difficulty and keep up with individual advancement.

The Deep rooted Excursion of Adaptability and Individual Advancement

Adaptability as a Deep rooted Pursuit

Adaptability isn't an objective however a deep rooted venture. As people progress through various phases of life, they experience new difficulties and open doors that require flexibility. Embracing adaptability as a nonstop pursuit guarantees continuous self-improvement and advancement.

Laying out Versatile Objectives

Versatile objective laying out includes making objectives that are adaptable and versatile. These objectives permit people to change their arrangements because of changing conditions while keeping a feeling of direction and heading.

The Continuous Development of Individual Advancement

Individual advancement is a dynamic, developing idea. What is progress today might contrast from tomorrow. People ought to constantly reconsider their qualities, needs,

and desires to guarantee that their quest for individual advancement stays lined up with their developing identity.

Assets for Proceeded with Development

The excursion of adaptability and individual advancement is improved by assets that help learning and advancement. These assets might incorporate books, courses, guides, and networks of similar people who share a guarantee to self-awareness.

1.1 The Power of Adaptability

In an always impacting world, the capacity to adjust isn't simply a worthwhile characteristic; it is the quintessence of endurance and progress. Mankind's set of experiences is loaded with accounts of civic establishments, species, and people who have flourished or died in view of their ability to adjust to moving conditions. In this investigation of the force of flexibility, we will dig into the crucial idea of variation, its importance in different areas of life, and the manners by which it enables people and social orders.

The Substance of Versatility

Transformation as a General Peculiarity

Transformation is a characteristic part of life itself. It is the capacity to change, adjust, or change because of new circumstances or conditions. Whether at the cell level, inside biological systems, or in the domain of human way of behaving, transformation is a general peculiarity that rises above limits.

The Darwinian Viewpoint

Charles Darwin's hypothesis of advancement by normal determination featured the focal job of variation in shaping life on The planet. Species that adjust effectively to their surroundings are bound to get by and imitate, giving their worthwhile characteristics to ensuing ages. This interaction highlights the significant effect of versatility on the variety and intricacy of living things.

Transformation in Nature

Nature's Show-stoppers of Transformation

The regular world is a mother lode of versatile wonders. From the chameleon's capacity to change its skin tone to the transient impulses of birds, transformation takes on horde structures in the set of all animals. These transformations are not unplanned yet are the consequence of millions of long periods of advancement, sharpened through the determined course of regular determination.

Environment Elements

Whole environments exhibit flexibility. When confronted with changes in environment, hunters, or accessible assets, biological systems change through complex communications among species. This flexibility guarantees the strength and steadiness of biological systems despite ecological movements.

Human Development and Social Transformation

Individuals, as well, are results of transformation. Our transformative excursion from old primates to current people is set apart by our ability to adjust truly, mentally, and socially. Our capacity to adjust to different conditions, make apparatuses, and foster complex social designs has empowered us to flourish in a large number of biological specialties.

Versatility In the public eye

Social and Social Variation

Society is a demonstration of human versatility. Our capacity to make and adjust to accepted practices, customs, and establishments has permitted us to assemble complex developments. As social orders change over the long run, they adjust to new mechanical, monetary, and social standards.

Mechanical Headways

Mechanical advancement is inseparable from flexibility. Developments that alter ventures and work on personal satisfaction are conceived out of the human ability to adjust to new difficulties and potential outcomes. From the print machine to the web, innovation is a demonstration of our capacity to shape and adjust to our general surroundings.

Financial Versatility

In the realm of financial matters, versatility is a foundation of flexibility. Organizations, businesses, and economies overall should adjust to vacillations in market interest, changes in customer inclinations, and troublesome advancements. Those that neglect

to adjust frequently face oldness, while versatile elements thrive.

The Versatile Outlook

The Development Mentality

At the singular level, flexibility is firmly connected to one's outlook. The idea of the "development attitude," promoted by analyst Hymn Dweck, underlines the conviction that capacities and knowledge can be created through exertion and learning. People

with a development mentality are bound to embrace difficulties, drive forward through mishaps, and adjust to evolving conditions.

Embracing Vulnerability

Versatility requires a level of solace with vulnerability. People who can explore vagueness and settle on choices in the midst of deficient data are more ready to confront the eccentricism of life. This ability to endure vulnerability is a sign of versatility.

Gaining from Disappointment

Disappointment is an inescapable piece of life, and flexibility frequently rises out of the examples learned through disappointment. Rather than survey disappointment as a loss, versatile people consider it to be a chance for development. They change their systems, refine their methodologies, and move ahead with recently discovered astuteness.

Variation in Self-improvement

Self-improvement and Flexibility

Self-improvement and flexibility are profoundly interlaced. To develop as people, we should adjust to changing conditions and embrace new difficulties. This might include gaining new abilities, moving viewpoints, or reexamining our objectives and needs.

Versatility Even with Misfortunes

Misfortunes are an inborn piece of the self-improvement venture. Whether in training, vocation, or connections, people who have flexibility are stronger despite mishaps. They view difficulties as impermanent snags and keep up with their obligation to advance.

Adjusting Objectives and Yearnings

Flexibility stretches out to the domain of objective setting. While laying out objectives is significant, it is similarly essential to adjust those objectives as conditions change. Adaptable objective setting permits people to stay lined up with their qualities and yearnings while changing their arrangements on a case by case basis.

Flexibility in Vocation and Expert Achievement

Vocation Adaptability

In the contemporary work market, profession adaptability is a valued resource. People who can adjust to new jobs, enterprises, and expertise requests have an upper hand. The capacity to learn and turn because of developing vocation scenes is crucial for long haul proficient achievement.

Business venture and Transformation

Business people represent versatility in the business world. They recognize open doors, foster creative arrangements, and turn their systems in light of market criticism. The capacity to adjust rapidly is much of the time a determinant of enterprising achievement.

Administration and Versatility

Successful administration requests flexibility. Pioneers who can change their administration styles to suit various circumstances and group elements are bound to move and guide their groups toward progress. Initiative is certainly not a one-size-fits-all undertaking, yet a versatile excursion.

The Job of Flexibility in Connections

Relational Adaptability

Solid connections require relational adaptability. People who can adjust their correspondence styles, understand others' viewpoints, and split the difference in clashes areas of strength for cultivate, connections. Relational flexibility supports common comprehension and association.

Compromise and Transformation

Clashes are unavoidable in any relationship, yet the way that they are settled relies upon flexibility. People who approach clashes with adaptability are bound to track down commonly good arrangements. They are available to think twice about ready to change their situations for the relationship's prosperity.

The Advancement of Connections

Connections advance after some time, and flexibility is fundamental for exploring these changes. Whether in heartfelt associations, kinships, or familial connections, flexibility permits people to oblige new life stages, obligations, and difficulties.

The Force of Flexibility in Testing Times

Transformation in Emergency

Testing times, for example, worldwide emergencies or individual difficulties, test one's flexibility without limit. People and networks that can adjust rapidly to startling misfortune are better situated to face the hardship and arise more grounded on the opposite side.

Flexibility Despite Affliction

Versatility upgrades flexibility in the midst of affliction. Strong people can adjust their survival methods, look for help, and find new wellsprings of solidarity while confronting testing conditions. This versatile flexibility is an incredible asset for defeating difficulty.

Illustrations from History

Since the beginning of time, flexibility plays had a crucial impact in human endurance and progress. From defeating cataclysmic events to answering financial emergencies, social orders that adjusted really have made due as well as changed difficulties into open doors for development and advancement.

Developing Flexibility

Fostering the Versatile Attitude

Developing versatility starts with cultivating a versatile outlook. This includes embracing change as a characteristic piece of life, seeing difficulties as any open doors, and keeping a development situated point of view.

Embracing Deep rooted Learning

Versatile people are deep rooted students. They effectively look for information, secure new abilities, and stay inquisitive about the world. Deep rooted learning isn't restricted to formal instruction however stretches out to casual encounters and independent investigation.

Building Flexibility

Flexibility is firmly interwoven with versatility. Building flexibility includes creating survival techniques, encouraging close to home prosperity, and developing an identity viability. Versatile people are more ready to adjust to difficulty.

Looking for Different Encounters

Openness to different encounters, societies, and viewpoints improves flexibility. Travel, chipping in, and drawing in with individuals from various foundations expand's comprehension one might interpret the world and cultivate versatility.

2 |

Chapter 2

The Science of Adaptability

Versatility is a crucial and complicated part of life. It is the capacity to change, alter, or change in light of new conditions or difficulties. While versatility is frequently connected with human way of behaving, it is, as a matter of fact, a general peculiarity that rises above species, biological systems, and, surprisingly, the sub-atomic designs of life. In this investigation of the study of flexibility, we will dive into the basic systems, transformative importance, neurological establishments, and mental parts of this striking characteristic that supports our endurance and progress.

The Transformative Foundations of Flexibility

The Darwinian System

The groundwork of flexibility can be followed back to Charles Darwin's hypothesis of development by normal choice. As per this system, people inside a populace shift in their characteristics, and those having worthwhile qualities have a superior possibility getting by and duplicating. Over the long haul, these characteristics become more predominant in the populace, prompting transformation to the climate.

Variation as the Main impetus

Variation is the main impetus behind the variety of life structures on The planet. It is through variation that species have advanced to possess essentially every environmental specialty, from the most profound seas to the most noteworthy mountains. This course of variation isn't restricted to enormous scope changes however stretches out to minute changes inside life forms at the hereditary level.

Microevolution and Macroevolution

Variation works at both microevolutionary and macroevolutionary scales. Microevolution alludes to limited scope changes in a populace's hereditary cosmetics over a brief period, like the improvement of anti-infection obstruction in microbes. Macroevolution, then again, incorporates bigger, long haul changes that lead to the development of new species.

Hereditary Transformation and Normal Determination Hereditary Variety

Hereditary transformation happens through the course of normal determination following up on hereditary variety inside a populace. Hereditary variety emerges from changes, hereditary recombination, and quality stream, making variety that normal choice can follow up on.

Regular Determination in real life

Directional Choice: Favors people with characteristics at one limit, prompting a change in the populace's normal qualities after some time.

Settling Choice: Favors people with middle of the road qualities, keeping up with the norm inside a populace.

Troublesome Choice: Favors people with outrageous qualities, possibly prompting the arrangement of two particular subpopulations.

Sexual Determination: Driven by mate decision, sexual choice frequently brings about the advancement of qualities that upgrade a person's conceptive achievement.

Human Development as an Exhibit

Human development gives a convincing exhibit of hereditary transformation. The advancement of bipedalism, the improvement of an enormous cerebrum, and the procurement of complex mental capacities are instances of versatile qualities that have molded our species.

The Job of Brain adaptability in Flexibility

The Mind's Versatile Limit

Brain adaptability, the mind's capacity to revamp itself by shaping new brain associations, is a foundation of flexibility. It permits the mind to change its construction and capability in light of learning, experience, and ecological changes.

Sorts of Brain adaptability

Underlying Pliancy: Includes actual changes in the cerebrum's construction, like the development of new neurons or the arrangement of new synaptic associations.

Practical Pliancy: Alludes to the mind's capacity to reallocate capabilities from harmed regions to whole areas, empowering recuperation from wounds or adjusting to new assignments.

Learning and Memory

Flexibility in learning and memory depends vigorously on brain adaptability. The development of recollections includes changes in synaptic strength, while the procurement of new abilities or information brings about the reworking of brain circuits.

Brain adaptability Across the Life expectancy

While the mind is generally plastic during early turn of events, it stays versatile over the course of life. The grown-up cerebrum can revamp in light of learning, recovery after wounds, and, surprisingly, ecological enhancement.

Mental Adaptability: Exploring Mental Scenes

Mental Adaptability Characterized

Mental adaptability is a particular part of flexibility that connects with one's capacity to switch between various mental errands or mental sets. It envelops innovativeness, critical thinking, and the ability to adjust to new data or evolving conditions.

Leader Capabilities and Mental Adaptability

The prefrontal cortex, especially the dorsolateral prefrontal cortex, assumes a focal part in leader capabilities, including mental adaptability. These capabilities include higher-request mental cycles, for example, independent direction, arranging, and critical thinking.

Improving Mental Adaptability

Mental Activities: Exercises like riddles, entertaining puzzles, and system games challenge mental adaptability.

Care and Contemplation: These practices energize receptiveness and the capacity to adjust one's reasoning.

Various Growth opportunities: Investigating new subjects, expressions, or abilities widens mental skylines and cultivates versatility.

The capacity to understand people on a profound level and Versatile Feelings

Profound Flexibility

Close to home flexibility is the ability to successfully explore and answer a great many feelings. It includes perceiving and controlling one's own feelings and understanding and identifying with the feelings of others.

The capacity to appreciate people on a profound level (EI)

Mindfulness: Remembering one's feelings and figuring out their effect.

Self-guideline: Overseeing and tweaking profound reactions, especially in upsetting circumstances.

Compassion: Understanding and sharing the feelings of others.

Interactive abilities: Exploring social circumstances and actually overseeing connections.

Feeling Guideline Procedures

Feeling guideline procedures, like mental reappraisal or care methods, enable people to adaptively deal with their feelings. These techniques can upgrade mental prosperity and relational connections.

Social Flexibility and Powerful Correspondence

Social Versatility

Social versatility includes the ability to change one's way of behaving, correspondence style, and cooperations to suit different social circumstances and settings. It assumes an essential part in building and keeping up with connections.

Successful Correspondence

Versatile correspondence is a foundation of social flexibility. Successful correspondence includes undivided attention, nonverbal signals, and the capacity to pass on messages obviously and empathically.

Relational Connections

Effective relational connections depend on friendly flexibility. The capacity to adjust to the requirements and inclinations of others cultivates shared figuring out, trust, and participation.

Versatility in Critical thinking and Navigation

Critical thinking Methodologies

Flexibility is essential in critical thinking. When stood up to with complex issues, people should have the option to create elective arrangements, adjust their methodologies, and assess the viability of various techniques.

Dynamic Under Vulnerability

Versatility is particularly significant in decision making when confronted with vulnerability. Versatile chiefs stay open to new data and change their decisions as conditions develop.

Versatility in Direction

Versatile chiefs display flexibility despite disappointments or misfortunes. As opposed to survey disappointments as losses, they use them as learning valuable chances to refine their dynamic cycles.

The Mental Parts of Flexibility

Versatile Methods for dealing with especially difficult times

Mental flexibility incorporates the capacity to adapt successfully to pressure, affliction, and life's difficulties. Versatile ways of dealing with hardship or stress include issue centered adapting, feeling centered adapting, and acknowledgment based adapting.

The Job of Good faith

Confidence, an inspirational perspective on what's to come, is firmly connected to versatility. Hopeful people are bound to see difficulties as reasonable and are better prepared to adjust to mishaps.

Flexibility and Versatility

Flexibility is a connected mental develop that converges with versatility. Strong people show flexibility in their ability to return from difficulty, gain from disappointments, and keep up with mental prosperity.

The Study of Versatility in Present day culture

Versatility in the Working environment

In the present quickly changing position market, versatility is a profoundly sought-after quality. Representatives who can adjust to new advances, work designs, and expertise prerequisites are bound to flourish in their professions.

Instructive Ideal models

Flexibility is progressively perceived as a crucial expertise in training. Present day instructive standards stress the improvement of decisive reasoning, critical thinking, and versatility to plan understudies for a unique future.

General Wellbeing and Pandemics

The Coronavirus pandemic featured the significance of flexibility at the cultural level. Countries that adjusted quickly to evolving conditions, for example, executing general wellbeing measures or changing to remote work, exhibited more prominent flexibility.

The Eventual fate of Flexibility: Difficulties and Open doors

Difficulties to Versatility

Protection from Change: Individuals frequently oppose change, which can upset flexibility.

Data Over-burden: In the computerized age, exploring a consistent convergence of data can overpower flexibility.

Social and Cultural Elements: Social standards and cultural designs can either advance or ruin flexibility.

Open doors for Improvement

Training: Consolidating versatility centered educational programs and instructing techniques.

Innovative Instruments: Utilizing innovation to work with learning and critical thinking.

Psychological wellness Drives: Advancing strength and the ability to appreciate people at their core.

2.1 Neuroplasticity and Personal Growth

The human cerebrum, with its mind boggling snare of neurons and neurotransmitters, is quite possibly of the most astounding and versatile organ in the body. It has the unprecedented ability to change and overhaul itself because of new encounters, difficulties, and learning open doors. This peculiarity, known as brain adaptability, assumes a significant part in self-improvement and improvement. In this investigation of brain adaptability and self-awareness, we will dig into the science behind this peculiarity, its effect on mental and profound turn of events, and functional methodologies to outfit its true capacity for extraordinary change.

Grasping Brain adaptability

Characterizing Brain adaptability

Brain adaptability, frequently alluded to as mind versatility, is the cerebrum's ability to surprise to rearrange its design, capabilities, and associations because of learning, experience, and ecological changes. It challenges the long-held conviction that the cerebrum's construction is fixed and unchangeable after a particular age.

The Verifiable Advancement of Brain adaptability

The idea of brain adaptability has developed over hundreds of years. Early hypotheses recommended that the mental health's was fixed during youth, however research in the twentieth century started to challenge these thoughts. Today, we comprehend that the cerebrum stays plastic over the course of life, ceaselessly adjusting to new conditions.

The Systems of Brain adaptability

Synaptic Pliancy

At the center of brain adaptability lies synaptic pliancy. This cycle includes changes in the strength and effectiveness of synaptic associations between neurons. Synaptic pliancy is liable for learning, memory arrangement, and expertise obtaining.

Long haul Potentiation (LTP) and Long haul Discouragement (LTD)

Two basic types of synaptic versatility are LTP and LTD. LTP reinforces synaptic associations, working with the transmission of signs between neurons, while LTD debilitates associations, lessening signal transmission. These cycles are vital for memory arrangement and learning.

Underlying Versatility

Notwithstanding synaptic pliancy, primary versatility includes actual changes in the cerebrum's construction. This incorporates the development of new neurons, the arrangement of new synaptic associations, and the pruning of unused associations. Primary versatility is especially applicable with regards to self-awareness and recuperation from cerebrum wounds.

Brain adaptability and Mental Development

Mental Development in Adulthood

In spite of prior convictions, mental development isn't restricted to youth and immaturity. Over the course of being an adult, the cerebrum can proceed to create and refine mental capabilities, for example, memory, critical thinking, and navigation.

Learning and Memory

Brain adaptability assumes a focal part in the development and combination of recollections. At the point when we master new data or abilities, the mind goes through changes in synaptic strength, empowering the encoding and recovery of recollections.

The Job of Involvement

Self-improvement frequently includes getting new information and abilities. Brain adaptability guarantees that encounters, whether through proper schooling or independent learning, are encoded in the mind's brain organizations.

Close to home Development and Brain adaptability

The capacity to appreciate individuals on a profound level

Profound development, portrayed by the capacity to appreciate individuals on a deeper level (EI), includes understanding and dealing with one's own feelings and relating to the feelings of others. Brain adaptability is vital to the improvement of the ability to understand anyone on a deeper level.

The Amygdala and Close to home Guideline

The amygdala, a key cerebrum structure engaged with close to home handling, shows brain adaptability. Through rehashed openness to profound encounters and guideline strategies, people can reshape the amygdala's reaction to close to home boosts.

Sympathy and Interactive abilities

Brain adaptability additionally supports the advancement of sympathy and interactive abilities. By rehearsing sympathy and taking part in significant social collaborations, people reinforce brain connections connected with social comprehension and close to home comprehension.

Defeating Difficulties and Building Versatility

Flexibility Notwithstanding Misfortune

Self-awareness frequently emerges from conquering difficulties and difficulty. Brain adaptability empowers people to adjust to and recuperate from troublesome encounters. Versatility, the capacity to quickly return from difficulties, is intently attached to brain adaptability.

Versatile Survival methods

Versatile methods for dealing with especially difficult times, like care, mental reappraisal, and acknowledgment based procedures, advance close to home guideline and upgrade strength. These systems can reshape brain circuits related with pressure reactions.

Post-Horrendous Development

At times, people experience post-horrendous development, a peculiarity where they rise up out of awful encounters with expanded individual strength and a more profound

feeling of importance. Brain adaptability assumes a critical part in working with this development.

Useful Systems to Upgrade Brain adaptability

Care and Reflection

Care works on, including reflection, advance brain adaptability by expanding dim matter thickness in cerebrum areas related with consideration, memory, and profound guideline. Standard care activities can upgrade mental and close to home development.

Actual Activity

Actual activity significantly affects brain adaptability. Oxygen consuming activity, specifically, advances the arrival of neurotrophic factors that help the development and upkeep of neurons. Practice additionally upgrades blood stream to the cerebrum, working with the conveyance of oxygen and supplements.

Sound Eating regimen and Nourishment

A decent eating regimen wealthy in cell reinforcements, omega-3 unsaturated fats, and different supplements upholds mind wellbeing and brain adaptability. These supplements give fundamental structure blocks to synaptic associations and synapse capability.

Ceaseless Learning and Scholarly Commitment

Participating in deep rooted realizing, whether through perusing, seeking after new leisure activities, or taking up instructive courses, animates brain adaptability. Scholarly commitment challenges the cerebrum and encourages mental development.

The Job of Brain adaptability in Private Change

Individual Change Characterized

Individual change addresses a significant and frequently deliberate change in one's convictions, values, ways of behaving, and personality. Brain adaptability is a basic instrument that works with individual change.

Bringing an end to Propensities and Laying out New Ones

Propensities, both positive and negative, are profoundly instilled brain designs. Brain adaptability permits people to bring an end to liberated from damaging things to do and make new, better ones by reshaping the brain processes related with these ways of behaving.

Personality and Mental self portrait

Individual change frequently includes a change in self-personality and mental self portrait. Brain adaptability permits people to rethink their self-idea, testing restricting convictions and developing a more sure and bona fide self-personality.

The Crossing point of Brain adaptability and Helpful Intercessions

Brain adaptability in Helpful Settings

Treatments intended to advance self-awareness and prosperity frequently influence brain adaptability. Mental conduct treatment (CBT), care based pressure decrease (MBSR), and rationalistic conduct treatment (DBT) are instances of helpful methodologies that saddle brain adaptability for close to home and social change.

Neurorehabilitation After Cerebrum Wounds

Brain adaptability is a foundation of recovery after mind wounds, like strokes or horrible cerebrum wounds (TBIs). Treatment programs are intended to assist patients with relearning lost abilities and adjust to their changed conditions.

Developing a Development Mentality

The Development Attitude Characterized

A development mentality is the conviction that capacities and insight can be created through exertion, learning, and constancy. This mentality adjusts intimately with the standards of brain adaptability and self-improvement.

Embracing Difficulties and Gaining from Disappointment

People with a development outlook embrace difficulties as any open doors for development and view disappointments as opportunities for growth. They are bound to persist through challenges, realizing that their endeavors add to self-awareness.

Developing a Development Outlook in Youngsters and Grown-ups

Encouraging a development mentality starts in youth however can be created at whatever stage in life. Guardians, teachers, and people themselves can develop this outlook through support, self-reflection, and purposeful practice.

2.2 Cognitive Flexibility

Mental adaptability is a mental expertise that permits people to adjust their reasoning and conduct because of changing circumstances and requests. A psychological readiness empowers us to move our mental cycles, viewpoints, and procedures when confronted with new data, difficulties, or errands. This limit is vital for critical thinking, navigation, imagination, and by and large flexibility in an always impacting world. In this

investigation of mental adaptability, we will dive into its definition, basic systems, formative viewpoints, and commonsense techniques to upgrade this fundamental mental ability.

Grasping Mental Adaptability

Characterizing Mental Adaptability

Mental adaptability is the capacity to switch between various mental errands, viewpoints, or mental sets when conditions change. It includes adjusting one's reasoning and conduct to satisfy the needs of a given circumstance. This expertise permits people to change flawlessly between various mental modes, like moving from centered consideration regarding inventive conceptualizing.

The Mental Adaptability Continuum

Mental adaptability exists on a continuum, going from inflexible reasoning and protection from change toward one side to exceptionally versatile, adaptable reasoning at the other. People might show changing levels of mental adaptability in various settings and circumstances.

The Systems of Mental Adaptability

Working Memory and Mental Control

Working memory, a transitory stockpiling framework for data and progressing mental cycles, assumes a basic part in mental adaptability. It empowers people to hold and control data, working with task-exchanging and variation.

Mental Control Cycles

Mental adaptability depends on mental control processes, for example, restraint and undertaking set moving. Restraint includes smothering superfluous data or prepotent reactions, while task-set moving includes progressing between various mental undertakings or mental sets.

Brain Premise of Mental Adaptability

Neuroimaging studies have recognized cerebrum districts related with mental adaptability, including the prefrontal cortex and the foremost cingulate cortex. These locales are engaged with observing, assessing, and changing mental cycles because of evolving requests.

Mental Adaptability Across the Life expectancy

Formative Parts of Mental Adaptability

Mental adaptability goes through critical advancement over the course of life. In youth, it is related with the development of leader capabilities and the prefrontal cortex. Puberty is set apart by expanded mental adaptability as people explore the intricacies of youth.

Adulthood and Maturing

Mental adaptability stays fundamental in adulthood, where it upholds flexibility in work, connections, and day to day existence. As people age, mental adaptability might decline, however it stays teachable and can be kept up with through mental commitment and long lasting learning.

The Job of Mental Adaptability in Critical thinking

Critical thinking Characterized

Critical thinking is a mental interaction that includes recognizing difficulties, creating possible arrangements, assessing their viability, and choosing the best strategy. Mental adaptability is a vital part of powerful critical thinking.

Dissimilar Reasoning and Inventiveness

Mental adaptability adds to dissimilar reasoning, a type of inventiveness that includes producing different answers for an issue. Imaginative people frequently display elevated degrees of mental adaptability, permitting them to investigate unpredictable thoughts and viewpoints.

Conquering Mental Unbending nature

Mental inflexibility, something contrary to mental adaptability, can impede critical thinking. At the point when people can't move their reasoning or consider elective arrangements, they might become trapped in useless critical thinking designs.

Mental Adaptability in Navigation

Decision Making as Mental Transformation

Navigation is an essential part of day to day existence, and mental adaptability assumes a critical part in going with versatile choices. People should change their dynamic procedures in view of changing data and objectives.

Dynamic Under Vulnerability

Mental adaptability is particularly important while going with choices under states of vulnerability. Versatile chiefs stay open to new data, change their methodologies, and consider elective choices as conditions advance.

Flexibility in Navigation

Mental adaptability improves strength in direction. When confronted with mishaps or horrible results, people with mental adaptability can reconsider their choices, gain from their encounters, and pursue more versatile decisions later on.

Improving Mental Adaptability

Care and Reflection

Care works on, including reflection, develop mental adaptability by advancing present-second mindfulness and non-critical perception of contemplations. Customary care activities can assist people with turning out to be more versatile in their reasoning.

Broadly educating Mental Abilities

Taking part in different mental exercises, like learning another dialect, playing instruments, or rehearsing various kinds of critical thinking puzzles, can broadly educate mental abilities and improve mental adaptability.

Embracing Oddity and Investigation

Searching out original encounters, difficulties, and viewpoints empowers mental adaptability. Heading out to new spots, attempting new exercises, or drawing in with individuals from assorted foundations animates versatile reasoning.

Mental Adaptability in Training and the Work environment

Instructive Ramifications

In training, cultivating mental adaptability is fundamental for getting ready understudies for the difficulties of the 21st 100 years. Educational plans that accentuate decisive reasoning, critical thinking, and interdisciplinary learning advance mental adaptability.

Work environment Pertinence

Mental adaptability is exceptionally pertinent in the work environment. In a quickly changing position market, representatives who can adjust to new advances, jobs, and obligations are bound to succeed. Bosses esteem versatile specialists who can explore dynamic workplaces.

Administration and The board

Compelling pioneers and administrators frequently display elevated degrees of mental adaptability. They can turn their systems, adjust to evolving conditions, and encourage development inside their groups.

The Impediments and Difficulties of Mental Adaptability

Individual Contrasts

Not all people have a similar degree of mental adaptability. Factors like hereditary qualities, childhood, and neurological circumstances can impact one's gauge level of mental adaptability.

Protection from Change

Mental adaptability can be provoked by protection from change, mental predispositions, or profound connections to existing convictions and viewpoints. Defeating these boundaries might require deliberate exertion and mindfulness.

Finding Some kind of harmony

While mental adaptability is significant, it isn't generally fitting or helpful in each circumstance. Finding some kind of harmony among versatility and soundness is fundamental for compelling independent direction and critical thinking.

The Fate of Mental Adaptability

Mental Adaptability in the Computerized Age

In the computerized age, the capacity to explore immense measures of data and adjust to quickly developing advances is vital. Mental adaptability will keep on assuming an essential part in successfully captivating with and utilizing computerized devices.

Schooling and Long lasting Learning

The fate of mental adaptability lies in training and deep rooted learning. As innovation and businesses advance, people should constantly refresh their abilities and adjust their reasoning to stay serious and significant.

Development and Critical thinking

Mental adaptability will drive development and critical thinking in different areas, including science, innovation, medical care, and business. Clever fixes to complex

worldwide difficulties will require versatile reasoning.

3

Chaptert 3

Embracing Change

Change is an intrinsic and steady part of human life and the world we occupy. It takes different structures, from individual changes and cultural movements to mechanical headways and natural changes. While change can be disrupting and testing, it is likewise a wellspring of development, advancement, and reestablishment. Embracing change is a key expertise and mentality that enables people and social orders to explore the extraordinary excursion of existence with strength, flexibility, and a feeling of direction. In this investigation of embracing change, we will dig into the definition and nature of progress, the mental and close to home elements of progress, systems for overseeing change successfully, and the significant effect of progress on private and aggregate development.

The Idea of Progress

Characterizing Change

Change is a unique cycle described by the modification, change, or progress from one state, circumstance, or condition to another. It envelops shifts in physical, mental, social, and natural parts of life.

The Certainty of Progress

Change is an inescapable and widespread part of human life. From the normal patterns of birth and passing to the advancement of social orders and civic establishments, change is an essential piece of the human experience.

The Assorted Types of Progress

Change takes assorted structures, including gradual and abrupt changes, individual and aggregate changes, and positive and testing changes. It can appear in different spaces, like connections, vocations, wellbeing, and innovation.

The Mental and Profound Components of Progress

The Mental Effect of Progress

Change frequently sets off mental reactions, including tension, vulnerability, and opposition. The level of mental effect relies upon elements like the idea of the change, individual survival strategies, and the degree of control people see over the change.

The Close to home Rollercoaster

Change is joined by a scope of feelings, from dread and misery to fervor and expectation. These feelings can vary all through the change cycle, making a close to home rollercoaster.

Protection from Change

Protection from change is a typical mental hindrance. People might oppose change because of dread of the obscure, connection to the recognizable, or worries about likely pessimistic outcomes. Understanding and tending to obstruction is fundamental for fruitful change the board.

The Phases of Progress

The Change Bend

Change frequently follows an anticipated example, known as the change bend. This model incorporates stages like disavowal, obstruction, investigation, and acknowledgment. Understanding these stages can assist people with exploring change all the more successfully.

Progress and Change

Change isn't just about outer changes yet additionally interior advances and changes. It includes relinquishing old characters, convictions, and propensities while embracing new ones.

The Job of Self-Reflection

Self-reflection is an important instrument for exploring change. It permits people to acquire experiences into their responses to change, recognize individual qualities and shortcomings, and put forth objectives for self-improvement.

Techniques for Overseeing Change Really
Developing Flexibility

Flexibility is the capacity to change and flourish in evolving conditions. Developing versatility includes fostering a development outlook, embracing learning potential open doors, and remaining open to new encounters.

Powerful Correspondence

Clear and compassionate correspondence is vital during seasons of progress. Pioneers, whether in private connections or associations, ought to impart the purposes behind change, its advantages, and the means in question. Open channels of correspondence assist people with feeling appreciated and comprehended.

Laying out Practical Objectives

Laying out clear and reachable objectives can give guidance and inspiration during seasons of progress. Objectives ought to be explicit, quantifiable, and time-bound, permitting people to keep tabs on their development and celebrate triumphs.

Building an Emotionally supportive network

An emotionally supportive network of companions, family, coaches, and partners can offer profound help, direction, and consolation during change. Social associations assume a significant part in flexibility and versatility.

The Force of Strength
Figuring out Strength

Flexibility is the capacity to quickly return from misfortune and keep up with mental prosperity. It includes adapting actually to pressure, misfortunes, and difficulties. Flexibility is firmly connected to embracing change.

Versatility Elements

A few variables add to strength, including an uplifting perspective, critical thinking abilities, a solid social encouraging group of people, and a feeling of direction. These variables can be developed and fortified over the long run.

Difficulty as an Impetus for Development

Affliction and change frequently remain closely connected. While difficulties can be troublesome, they additionally give open doors to self-awareness, self-disclosure, and the improvement of versatility.

Change and Self-awareness

Change as an Impetus for Self-awareness

Change can possibly invigorate self-awareness and improvement. It moves people to adjust, learn, and gain new abilities and viewpoints. Embracing have an impact on with a development outlook can prompt extraordinary self-awareness.

Rehash and Change

Change offers people the potential chance to rethink themselves and seek after new interests, vocations, or life ways. Change includes shedding old personalities and embracing new ones that line up with one's developing qualities and yearnings.

Embracing Vulnerability

Change frequently brings vulnerability, and figuring out how to embrace vulnerability is a significant expertise. It includes relinquishing the requirement for outright control and confiding in one's capacity to adjust and make the best of advancing conditions.

Change In the public eye and Culture

The Elements of Cultural Change

Social orders and societies additionally experience change on different scales. Social change envelops shifts in standards, values, customs, and establishments. It very well may be progressive or quick, determined by variables like mechanical headways, segment shifts, or political developments.

Obstruction and Transformation

Cultural change frequently meets with obstruction from people and gatherings who try to safeguard the state of affairs. Nonetheless, social orders likewise have a surprising limit with respect to transformation and development because of evolving conditions.

Aggregate Development and Progress

Change at the cultural level can prompt aggregate development and progress. It can bring about better day to day environments, more prominent correspondence, and extended open doors for people and networks.

The Effect of Innovative Change

The Speed increase of Mechanical Change

Mechanical progressions are a critical driver of progress in the cutting edge world. The quick speed of innovative change has changed enterprises, economies, correspondence, and day to day existence.

Adjusting to Mechanical Change

Embracing innovative change includes remaining informed about arising advances, securing computerized education abilities, and perceiving the expected advantages and dangers. It additionally requires adjusting to advancing workplaces and profession requests.

Moral Contemplations

Innovative change brings up moral issues connected with protection, security, imbalance, and the effect of robotization on work. Society should explore these moral difficulties while outfitting innovation's true capacity for positive change.

The Fate of Progress

The Speed increase of Progress

The speed of progress is supposed to advance quickly from here on out, driven by elements, for example, man-made consciousness, biotechnology, environmental change, and worldwide interconnectedness.

People and social orders should adjust to progressively unique and capricious circumstances.

Flexibility and Maintainability

Embracing change later on will require an emphasis on flexibility and maintainability. Versatile people and networks will be better prepared to answer startling difficulties, while manageability endeavors will address long haul ecological and social changes.

Development and Innovativeness

Change encourages development and innovativeness, which will keep on being fundamental for tackling complex worldwide issues. Empowering innovativeness and encouraging a culture of development will be significant for tending to the difficulties representing things to come.

3.1 The Nature of Change

Change is an inborn and unavoidable power that shapes the actual texture of our reality. From the subatomic particles that dance and change in the universe to the terrific transformative movements that have brought about existence on The planet, change is woven into the embroidery of the universe. It influences each part of our lives, from the individual changes we go through to the cultural, mechanical, and ecological changes that characterize our time. In this investigation of the idea of progress, we will dive into its crucial qualities, the job it plays in various areas, the science behind it, and the significant ramifications it holds for how we might interpret the world and ourselves.

Characterizing Change

The Embodiment of Progress

Change can be characterized as the method involved with progressing from one state, condition, or circumstance to another. It envelops modifications, changes, and changes in different parts of presence, including physical, organic, mental, and social domains.

Dynamic and Inescapable

Change is both dynamic and inescapable. It is an inherent element of the universe, and there is nothing left static or perpetual over the long haul. Whether on an infinite scale or inside the minutest particles, change is ever-present.

The General Rule of Progress

The Bolt of Time

Change is frequently connected with the idea of time. It unfurls in a directional way, moving from past to present to future. This bolt of time brings about the unfurling of occasions and the movement of history.

Entropy and Turmoil

The second law of thermodynamics expresses that in disengaged frameworks, entropy, or turmoil, will in general increment over the long haul. This guideline highlights the regular propensity of frameworks to advance, change, and eventually crumble.

Change in Grandiose Scales

The actual universe is in a condition of steady change. Stars are conceived and bite the dust, worlds impact and consolidation, and the universe extends. These grandiose changes have significant ramifications for the development of universes, stars, and planets.

Change in the Actual World

The Dance of Particles

At the most basic level, change is obvious in the way of behaving of subatomic particles. Quantum mechanics uncovers a unique reality where particles are continually moving, interfacing, and changing.

Actual Regulations and Constants

The crucial constants of the universe, like the speed of light or the gravitational steady, are not changeless however may fluctuate over infinite timescales. This variety has suggestions for the solidness of actual regulations.

Cosmological Change

The actual universe is likely to change on a cosmological scale. The Theory of prehistoric cosmic detonation portrays a sensational occasion that noticeable the introduction of the universe, starting a continuous course of grandiose extension and development.

Natural Development and Change
The Tree of Life

Natural development is a demonstration of the force of progress. Life on Earth has developed more than billions of years through the course of normal determination, bringing about the variety of species and the rise of mind boggling creatures.

Transformation and Endurance

Change in the organic domain is driven by variation to evolving conditions. Life forms that can adjust to new circumstances have a superior opportunity of endurance and multiplication, giving their worthwhile characteristics to people in the future.

Human Development

The account of human development mirrors our species' ability for change and variation. From our earliest precursors to present day people, we have constantly developed truly, intellectually, and socially.

Mental Change and Human Turn of events
Mental Turn of events

Change is fundamental to human turn of events and mental development. From outset to advanced age, people go through significant mental changes in regions like comprehension, feeling, and social connections.

Mental Turn of events

Piaget's hypothesis of mental advancement features how youngsters progress through particular phases of mental change, each set apart by shifts in thinking, critical abilities to think, and comprehension of the world.

Personality and Self-Idea

Mental change reaches out to the arrangement of one's character and self-idea. Puberty, specifically, is a period set apart by huge personality investigation and change.

Cultural Change and Social Advancement
Social and Social Changes

Change isn't restricted to the individual; it stretches out to social orders and societies. Mankind's set of experiences is set apart by cultural changes, remembering shifts for administration, innovation, financial matters, and social qualities.

Mechanical Headways

Mechanical change has been a main impetus behind cultural change. Developments, for example, the print machine, steam motor, and the web have reshaped human social orders and societies.

Social Advancement

Social change happens through a course of social development, where thoughts, convictions, practices, and innovations are sent, adjusted, and adjusted over ages. This unique interaction shapes social variety and advancement.

The Profound Scene of Progress

Profound Reactions to Change

Change frequently inspires a scope of close to home reactions. These may incorporate energy and expectation, nervousness and dread, trouble and sadness, or a mind boggling blend of feelings.

The Brain research of Versatility

Versatility is the capacity to adjust and return quickly from misfortune. Understanding and developing strength can assist people with exploring the inner difficulties of progress effortlessly.

Acknowledgment and Adapting

Acknowledgment is a vital mental expertise in embracing change. Recognizing the truth of progress, regardless of whether it is unwanted, is the most important move toward viable adapting and transformation.

The Study of Progress: Disorder Hypothesis and Intricacy

Tumult Hypothesis

Tumult hypothesis investigates the way of behaving of dynamic frameworks that are profoundly delicate to starting circumstances. Little changes in beginning circumstances can prompt radically various results, outlining the erratic idea of certain changes.

Intricacy Science

Intricacy science inspects how complex frameworks, like environments, economies, and social orders, change and adjust. These frameworks show rising ways of behaving that outcome from connections among their parts.

Nonlinear Elements

Nonlinear elements, a vital idea in figuring out change, depicts how little data sources or bothers can prompt nonlinear, unbalanced changes in a framework. This can bring about unforeseen and extraordinary results.

Exploring Change: Procedures and Mentalities

Versatility and Adaptability

Versatility is the ability to change in accordance with new circumstances and conditions. Embracing change frequently requires adaptability in thinking and conduct.

Versatility and Adapting

Versatility includes the capacity to return quickly from mishaps and misfortune. Survival techniques, for example, critical thinking, looking for help, and keeping an inspirational perspective, are fundamental instruments for exploring change.

Learning and Development Mentality

A development mentality, portrayed by a confidence in one's capacity to learn and develop, encourages a positive way to deal with change. Embracing change as a chance for learning and self-awareness can prompt extraordinary encounters.

The Significant Ramifications of Embracing Change

Self-awareness and Change

Embracing change makes the way for self-awareness and change. It moves people to adjust, learn, and develop, prompting more noteworthy mindfulness and flexibility.

Development and Progress

Change is an impetus for development and progress in different spaces, including science, innovation, and human expression. It drives human innovativeness and the improvement of groundbreaking thoughts and arrangements.

Cultural and Social Headway

Cultural and social change can prompt advancement and headways in regions like social equality, orientation fairness, and civil rights. Embracing change is much of the time a main impetus behind these positive changes.

The Eventual fate of Progress: Difficulties and Open doors

Speeding up Change

The speed of progress in the cutting edge world is speeding up, driven by mechanical headways, globalization, and interconnectedness. This presents the two difficulties and open doors for people and social orders.

Moral Contemplations

As change unfurls, moral contemplations become progressively significant. Choices connected with ecological supportability, civil rights, and mechanical improvement have expansive results.

Versatile Authority

Pioneers in different spaces, from legislative issues to business, should embrace versatile administration, which includes exploring change, cultivating development, and advancing flexibility inside associations and networks.

3.2 Building Resilience

Versatility is a wonderful human quality that enables people to quickly return from difficulty, face life's difficulties with boldness, and flourish notwithstanding mishaps. It's the capacity to endure affliction, adjust to change, and develop further simultaneously. Versatility is certainly not a natural characteristic yet an expertise that can be created and sustained after some time. In this investigation of building versatility, we will dive into the definition and significance of flexibility, the key parts that make up strength, methodologies to develop flexibility in people and networks, and the groundbreaking effect of strength on emotional well-being and prosperity.

Characterizing Flexibility

The Quintessence of Flexibility

Strength can be characterized as the ability to endure and bounce back from misfortune, adjust decidedly to change, and arise more grounded from testing educational encounters. A dynamic and developing quality permits people to explore life's high points and low points with effortlessness.

The Complex Idea of Strength

Versatility incorporates different aspects, including profound strength (adapting to feelings), mental flexibility (mental adaptability and critical thinking), social strength (encouraging groups of people and connections), and actual flexibility (wellbeing and prosperity).

The Significance of Flexibility

Flourishing in Affliction

Versatility is critical for flourishing even with affliction. It engages people to keep up with their psychological and profound prosperity in any event, when stood up to with life's most difficult conditions.

Upgrading Emotional wellness

Strength is firmly connected to emotional wellness. People with more elevated levels of strength are better prepared to oversee pressure, nervousness, and sorrow, prompting worked on by and large mental prosperity.

Transformation to Change

In a steadily impacting world, strength is fundamental for adjusting to new conditions, exploring advances, and embracing self-awareness amazing open doors.

The Parts of Versatility

Close to home Guideline

Close to home strength includes perceiving, understanding, and really dealing with one's feelings. It incorporates survival methods to manage pressure, uneasiness, and misery while keeping up with close to home equilibrium.

Positive Reasoning

Mental versatility fixates on fostering an uplifting perspective and keeping up with mental adaptability. It includes reexamining negative contemplations, looking for potential open doors for development, and supporting a development mentality.

Social Help

Social versatility depends on strong connections and associations with others. A hearty informal organization offers close to home help, assets, and a feeling of having a place.

Actual Wellbeing and Prosperity

Actual strength is intently attached to generally speaking wellbeing and prosperity. A sound way of life, including legitimate nourishment, exercise, and rest, improves one's capacity to adapt to difficulty.

Systems for Building Versatility

Care and Reflection

Care works on, including reflection, develop profound guideline and mental clearness. They assist people with remaining present at the time and foster mindfulness.

Stress The executives

Powerful pressure the executives methods, for example, unwinding works out, profound breathing, and using time productively, assist with diminishing the effect of weight on mental and close to home prosperity.

Critical thinking Abilities

Creating solid critical thinking abilities enables people to move toward difficulties with an answer situated mentality. Recognizing expected arrangements and making a conclusive move encourages a feeling of control.

Social Association

Assembling and sustaining steady connections is fundamental for social flexibility. Keeping up with associations with companions, family, and a local area gives a security net during troublesome times.

Building Flexibility in Youngsters and Teenagers

The Job of Life as a youngster Encounters

Youth encounters assume a huge part in forming flexibility. A stable and sustaining climate, positive good examples, and open doors for freedom and dominance add to the improvement of flexibility in youngsters.

Showing The capacity to understand people on a deeper level

Showing kids the ability to understand people on a profound level, including perceiving and dealing with their feelings, helps fabricate close to home strength. It empowers them to actually explore social circumstances.

Empowering Critical thinking Abilities

Cultivating critical thinking abilities in kids supports independence and self-adequacy. It sets them up to handle life's difficulties with certainty.

Building Versatility in Networks

Local area Emotionally supportive networks

Networks can construct versatility through emotionally supportive networks, for example, debacle readiness plans, guiding administrations, and nearby assets. These frameworks offer a security net during emergencies.

Schooling and Mindfulness

Instructive drives that advance strength mindfulness and adapting abilities inside networks can enable people to by and large face affliction.

Enabling Weak Populaces

Endeavors to engage weak populaces, like low-pay families, outcasts, or people with handicaps, add to local area versatility. Giving assets, potential open doors, and social help can have a massive effect.

The Extraordinary Effect of Flexibility

Self-awareness and Improvement

Flexibility isn't just about quickly returning; it's tied in with bobbing forward. The individuals who develop versatility frequently experience significant self-awareness, expanded mindfulness, and a more profound feeling of direction.

Defeating Injury and Affliction

Versatility enables people to conquer injury and difficulty, permitting them to reconstruct their lives and recover a feeling of control and reason.

Advancing Positive Psychological well-being

A versatile outlook is a foundation of positive emotional wellness. Strength furnishes people with the apparatuses they need to oversee pressure, adapt to difficulties, and keep up with close to home prosperity.

Strength Notwithstanding Worldwide Difficulties

Pandemics and Wellbeing Emergencies

Strength has been scrutinized during worldwide wellbeing emergencies like the Coronavirus pandemic. People, people group, and countries have needed to adjust, conquer difficulties, and show strength notwithstanding vulnerability.

Natural Difficulties

Environmental change and cataclysmic events require an aggregate versatility reaction. Building strong networks and supportable practices is fundamental for relieving the effect of ecological difficulties.

Social and Financial Imbalances

Versatility is basic for tending to social and monetary imbalances. Engaging underestimated populaces to fabricate strength can assist with spanning these incongruities.

The Fate of Versatility

Adjusting to a Questionable Future

As the world turns out to be more interconnected and dynamic, flexibility will assume a significantly more pivotal part in assisting people and networks with adjusting to a questionable future.

Innovation and Versatility

Innovation offers open doors for building strength, from inventive catastrophe reaction frameworks to telehealth administrations for emotional well-being support.

Worldwide Joint effort

In an undeniably interconnected world, worldwide cooperation on strength building endeavors will be fundamental. Countries and associations can gain from one another's encounters and techniques for building versatility.

4

Chapter 4

Flexible Goal Setting

Objective setting is a principal part of individual and expert turn of events. It gives a guide to accomplishment and enables people to understand their yearnings. Notwithstanding, unbending or unreasonable objectives can prompt disappointment and ruin progress. Interestingly, adaptable objective setting includes setting clear targets while staying open to changes and changes en route. It permits people to adjust to developing conditions, gain from difficulties, and eventually make progress. In this investigation of adaptable objective setting, we will dive into the definition and meaning of adaptable objective setting, the brain science behind it, viable techniques for execution, and genuine instances of its effect on private and expert achievement.

The Pith of Adaptable Objective Setting

Understanding Objective Setting

Objective setting is the most common way of characterizing explicit, quantifiable goals that one intends to accomplish inside a characterized time period. Objectives give guidance, inspiration, and a feeling of direction.

The Entanglements of Unbending Objective Setting

While defining objectives is fundamental, unbending objective setting can be counterproductive. Unreachable objectives or an unyielding methodology can prompt disappointment, stress, and burnout.

The Versatile Methodology

Adaptable objective setting, then again, joins the advantages of objective setting with versatility. It permits people to adjust their objectives in light of evolving conditions, misfortunes, or new open doors.

The Brain science of Objective Setting

The Inspiration Driving Objectives

Objectives act as strong inspirations. They make a feeling of direction and heading, driving people to make a move and persist through difficulties.

The Job of Self-Assurance

Self-assurance hypothesis features the significance of independence and characteristic inspiration in objective pursuit. Adaptable objective setting lines up with self-assurance by permitting people to simply decide and keep up with their natural inspiration.

The Effect of Objective Setting on Prosperity

Research shows that laying out and taking a stab at significant objectives adds to a feeling of prosperity and life fulfillment. Adaptable objective setting can upgrade prosperity by lessening pressure and expanding versatility.

The Advantages of Adaptable Objective Setting

Flexibility and Strength

Adaptable objective setting upgrades flexibility and versatility. At the point when people are available to changing their objectives, misfortunes are viewed as learning valuable open doors instead of disappointments.

Stress Decrease

Adaptable objective setting decreases pressure by permitting people to adjust to evolving conditions. This adaptability forestalls the dissatisfaction and nervousness that can result from unbendingly chasing after unreachable objectives.

Expanded Innovativeness and Advancement

Adaptability in objective setting empowers imaginative reasoning and advancement. It permits people to investigate elective methodologies and answers for accomplish their goals.

Down to earth Procedures for Adaptable Objective Setting

Defining Brilliant Objectives

Brilliant objectives are Explicit, Quantifiable, Attainable, Significant, and Time-bound. By applying these standards, people make clear and sensible objectives that can be adjusted depending on the situation.

Laying out Achievements

Breaking bigger objectives into more modest, reasonable achievements gains ground more unmistakable and considers ordinary reassessment and change.

Focusing on Values

Adjusting objectives to individual qualities guarantees that they stay significant and spurring. At the point when objectives mirror one's qualities, people are bound to adjust and continue.

Genuine Instances of Adaptable Objective Setting

Business

In the unique universe of business venture, adaptable objective setting is fundamental. Effective business people frequently adjust their business systems and goals in light of market changes and client criticism.

Professional success

In the expert domain, adaptable objective setting can prompt professional success. Workers who are available to changing their vocation objectives in light of new open doors or ability improvement are bound to make progress.

Self-improvement

On an individual level, adaptable objective setting adds to self-improvement. People chasing after wellbeing and wellness objectives, for example, can adjust their schedules and targets as they dive more deeply into their bodies and inclinations.

Difficulties and Hindrances in Adaptable Objective Setting

Anxiety toward Disappointment

The feeling of dread toward disappointment can be a huge obstruction in adaptable objective setting. People might oppose changing their objectives to try not to recognize difficulties or saw disappointments.

Outside Tensions

Outside pressures, for example, cultural assumptions or companion impacts, can block adaptable objective setting. People might feel a sense of urgency to stick to inflexible targets to live up to others' assumptions.

Absence of Mindfulness

Successful adaptable objective setting requires mindfulness. A few people might battle with mindfulness, making it trying to adjust their objectives in arrangement with their developing requirements and goals.

Conquering Difficulties and Building Versatility

Developing a Development Outlook

A development outlook is the conviction that capacities and insight can be created through exertion and learning. Embracing a development outlook urges people to see difficulties as any open doors for development.

Rehearsing Self-Empathy

Self-empathy includes treating oneself with graciousness and figuring out, particularly in snapshots of trouble. It assists people with beating the apprehension about disappointment and adjust to evolving conditions.

Looking for Help and Responsibility

Having an emotionally supportive network or a responsibility accomplice can give consolation and direction in adaptable objective setting. These people can offer points of view and bits of knowledge that work with versatility.

The Convergence of Adaptable Objective Setting and Prosperity

Lessening Pressure and Tension

Adaptable objective setting decreases pressure and uneasiness related with unbending objective pursuit. People who can change their objectives in light of life's unpredictabilities enjoy more prominent harmony of brain.

Upgrading Life Fulfillment

At the point when people put forth and adjust their objectives in arrangement with their qualities and developing goals, they experience expanded life fulfillment and a feeling of satisfaction.

Advancing Positive Connections

Adaptable objective setting can further develop connections by permitting people to focus on significant investment for their friends and family, decreasing contentions that might emerge from unbending objective pursuit.

The Fate of Adaptable Objective Setting

Developments in Objective Setting Innovation

Progressions in innovation, for example, man-made consciousness and customized objective setting applications, will offer new devices and experiences for adaptable objective setting.

Work environment Adaptability

As work environments advance, adaptable objective setting will turn out to be significantly more basic. Managers will perceive the significance of versatility and independence in objective setting for worker prosperity and efficiency.

Instructive Movements

Adaptable objective setting will likewise assume part in training. Schools and instructive organizations will zero in on fostering understudies' versatility, imagination, and critical thinking abilities.

4.1 Setting and Adjusting Goals

Objective setting is an essential part of human undertaking, giving guidance, reason, and inspiration. Whether in self-improvement, proficient turn of events, or any everyday issue, setting clear targets helps people imagine and make progress toward their ideal future. In any case, objective setting is certainly not a static cycle. It requires a level of flexibility and a comprehension that life is loaded up with turns, turns, and unforeseen difficulties. In this investigation of laying out and changing objectives, we will dig into the specialty of creating significant objectives, the study of powerful objective setting, methodologies for accomplishing them, and the significance of adaptability chasing our fantasies.

The Embodiment of Objective Setting

Understanding Objective Setting

Objective setting is the most common way of recognizing explicit, quantifiable targets that one intends to accomplish inside a characterized time period. It fills in as a guide for progress and gives a feeling of motivation and bearing.

The Inspiration Driving Objectives

Objectives go about as strong inspirations. They make a need to get moving and responsibility, rousing people to make a move and conquer deterrents on their way to accomplishment.

Sorts of Objectives

Objectives can be ordered into different sorts, including present moment and long haul objectives, result based objectives, and cycle based objectives. Each type fills an alternate need and offers one of a kind advantages.

The Brain research of Objective Setting

The Force of Expectation

Laying out clear objectives enacts the reticular actuating framework (RAS) in the mind, which upgrades consciousness of chances and assets that line up with one's targets.

Objective Direction

Objective direction alludes to a singular's way to deal with objective pursuit. It very well may be execution situated, where achievement is characterized by accomplishing the best result, or authority arranged, where achievement is estimated by self-awareness and learning.

Self-Assurance Hypothesis

Self-assurance hypothesis underlines the significance of independence, ability, and relatedness in objective setting. It features that objectives lined up with one's inherent inspirations are bound to actually be sought after.

Creating Significant Objectives

Savvy Objectives

The Savvy models - Explicit, Quantifiable, Feasible, Significant, and Time-bound - give an organized structure to creating significant objectives. Savvy objectives explain targets and make them significant.

The Force of Lucidity

Obviously characterizing objectives is fundamental for understanding the ideal result and the means expected to accomplish it. Vagueness in objective setting can prompt disarray and decreased inspiration.

The Job of Values

Adjusting objectives to individual qualities guarantees that they are significant and rousing. Values-based objective setting associates the quest for goals to one's center convictions and standards.

Techniques for Successful Objective Setting

Picturing Achievement

Representation is a useful asset for objective setting. It includes intellectually practicing the method involved with accomplishing an objective, upgrading inspiration and self-assurance.

Separating Objectives

Breaking bigger objectives into more modest, reasonable advances increments lucidity and works with progress following. These more modest achievements make the way to accomplishment more attainable.

Using time productively and Prioritization

Successful using time productively and prioritization are vital for objective accomplishment. People should assign time and assets to their objectives in arrangement with their significance.

Difficulties in Objective Setting

Overambitious Objectives

Putting forth excessively aggressive objectives that are past one's ongoing capacities can prompt dissatisfaction and burnout. Finding some kind of harmony among testing and feasible objectives is fundamental.

Hesitation and Interruptions

Hesitation and interruptions can wreck objective pursuit. Conquering these difficulties requires discipline, using time productively, and systems for keeping up with center.

Anxiety toward Failure*

The anxiety toward disappointment can deaden people and keep them from laying out and chasing after objectives. Developing a development mentality that sees disappointment as a venturing stone to progress can assist with relieving this trepidation.

The Significance of Adaptability

Perceiving the Requirement for Change

Definitely, conditions change, and deterrents emerge that require objective changes. Perceiving the requirement for adaptability and versatility is vital to long haul achievement.

Gaining from Setbacks*

Mishaps and disappointments are not disappointments of objective setting yet valuable open doors for development and learning. Adaptable people view misfortunes as input and change their methodology as needs be.

Turning versus Leaving Goals*

There is a qualification among turning and leaving objectives. Turning includes changing the procedure while keeping up with the center goal, while leaving objectives implies perceiving that the first goal is at this point not practical.

Procedures for Changing Objectives

Consistent Monitoring*

Consistently exploring progress toward objectives permits people to recognize deterrents and change their methodologies appropriately. Checking gives experiences into what is working and what needs change.

Input and Adaptation*

Looking for criticism from friends, tutors, or specialists can give important points of view and suggestions for objective change. Transformation is a proactive reaction to input.

Setting New Goals*

At the point when conditions change fundamentally or when objectives are as of now not significant, putting forth new objectives becomes vital. New objectives ought to line up with one's developing needs and goals.

Genuine Instances of Defining and Changing Objectives

Profession Advancement*

In the expert domain, laying out and changing objectives are normal practices. Experts frequently adjust their vocation goals in view of changing economic situations, industry patterns, and self-improvement.

Entrepreneurship*

Business visionaries often explore a powerful scene where flexibility and objective change are basic for business achievement. Moving business sector requests or startling difficulties might require new techniques and goals.

Individual Development*

In self-awareness, people frequently refine their objectives as they gain clearness about their qualities, interests, and life conditions. This flexibility guarantees that objectives stay applicable and rousing.

Adjusting Determination and Adaptability

The Job of Perseverance*

Constancy is vital for accomplishing testing objectives. It includes industriousness, flexibility, and the eagerness to conquer impediments and mishaps.

The Specialty of Knowing When to Adjust*

Adjusting steadiness and adaptability requires insight. It includes perceiving when conditions or criticism demonstrate the requirement for objective change.

Instinct and Self-Reflection*

Instinct and self-reflection are fundamental apparatuses for measuring the fittingness of changes. Paying attention to one's internal insight and assessing self-awareness are key parts of powerful objective setting.

4.2 Success Stories in Goal Adaptation

Achievement is in many cases depicted as a direct excursion, with clear objectives prompting clear achievements. Truly, achievement is regularly accomplished through flexibility, versatility, and the capacity to change and turn when confronted with surprising difficulties. In this investigation of examples of overcoming adversity in objective variation, we will dig into the moving excursions of people who confronted mishaps, reclassified their targets, and eventually accomplished their fantasies. These accounts represent the force of adaptability and flexibility chasing after progress, showing the way that mishaps can act as venturing stones as opposed to barricades.

The Force of Flexibility

The Narrative of J.K. Rowling

One of the most famous instances of objective variation is J.K. Rowling, the creator of the Harry Potter series. Rowling confronted various dismissals from distributers before her most memorable book was acknowledged. Her excursion to progress was set apart by private battles, including neediness and the deficiency of her mom. Regardless of these difficulties, she adjusted her objectives and drove forward, eventually becoming one of the world's top of the line creators.

Key Focus point: Flexibility and versatility can assist people with conquering dismissal and misfortune on their way to progress.

Embracing Change

The Change of Nokia

Nokia, when a goliath in the cell phone industry, confronted a precarious downfall when cell phones disturbed the market. Instead of gripping to their current objectives, Nokia adjusted by pulling together on media communications foundation and organization innovation. This essential shift permitted them to remain important and prevail in an alternate area of the business.

Key Action item: Embracing change and being available to changing objectives can prompt new open doors and supported achievement.

Turning for Advancement

The Excursion of Instagram

Instagram started as an area based social registration application called Burbn. The originators perceived the stage's photograph sharing component was acquiring prominence and chose to turn, rebranding as Instagram. This transformation prompted its touchy development, making it a main web-based entertainment stage.

Key Action item: Recognizing arising patterns and adjusting objectives to gain by them can prompt advancement and achievement.

From Misfortunes to Strength

The Victory of Oprah Winfrey

Oprah Winfrey confronted various difficulties in her initial life, including destitution and misuse. In spite of these difficulties, she persisted and adjusted her objectives to turn into an effective moderator, news magnate, and humanitarian. Her process shows the extraordinary force of versatility and flexibility.

Key Focal point: Adjusting objectives because of affliction can prompt self-awareness and exceptional accomplishments.

Transforming Mishaps into Open doors

The Versatility of Walt Disney

Walt Disney confronted various difficulties, including insolvency and the deficiency of protected innovation freedoms. In any case, he adjusted his objectives and persistently sought after his vision of making a supernatural diversion realm. His versatility prompted the formation of Disneyland and the getting through tradition of Disney.

Key Important point: Misfortune can be an impetus for rethinking objectives and making long haul progress.

The Force of Persistent Learning

The Development of Amazon

Amazon started as an internet based book shop yet developed into an online business monster that offers a large number of items and administrations. Jeff Bezos, the pioneer, stressed constant learning and a client driven approach. His versatility and readiness to turn added to Amazon's prosperity.

Key Focal point: Embracing a learning mentality and being willing to turn can drive long haul achievement and development.

Adjusting to Market Changes
The Tale of Netflix

Netflix began as a DVD rental help yet adjusted its objectives while streaming innovation arose. By moving its concentration to web based streaming, Netflix turned into a worldwide diversion force to be reckoned with, reforming the manner in which individuals consume content.

Key Action item: Market changes can set out open doors for objective transformation and development.

Utilizing Criticism and Information
The Outcome of Airbnb

Airbnb pioneers Brian Chesky, Nathan Blecharczyk, and Joe Gebbia adjusted their objectives in view of client criticism and information. Initially a stage for leasing pneumatic beds, Airbnb changed into a worldwide excursion rental commercial center, embracing versatility and development.

Key Focal point: Standing by listening to client input and utilizing information can direct viable objective variation.

Adjusting to Self-improvement
The Change of Elon Musk

Elon Musk, the business person behind organizations like SpaceX and Tesla, adjusted his objectives as his inclinations and abilities advanced. From helping to establish PayPal to seeking after aggressive space investigation and electric vehicle objectives, Musk's flexibility has driven his prosperity.

Key Focal point: Self-improvement can prompt advancing objectives that line up with one's interests and gifts.

Chapter 5

Career Flexibility

In the present quickly developing position market and working environment scene, vocation adaptability has turned into a pivotal resource for people meaning to flourish in their expert lives. Gone are the times of direct vocation ways and professional stability. All things considered, versatility, strength, and the capacity to turn are the keys to progress. In this far reaching investigation of profession adaptability, we will dive into the definition and meaning of vocation adaptability, the changing idea of work, procedures for creating vocation flexibility, genuine instances of adaptable profession ways, and the eventual fate of work in a time of constant change.

Characterizing Vocation Adaptability

Grasping Vocation Adaptability

Vocation adaptability alludes to a singular's ability to adjust, change, and pursue informed decisions in their expert process. It incorporates the capacity to turn, take on new jobs, and develop as the gig market and individual conditions change.

The Customary versus Adaptable Profession Worldview

Customary vocation ways frequently followed a straight direction, with people ascending a progressive stepping stool inside a solitary association. Conversely, an adaptable vocation worldview perceives that profession ways are progressively non-straight, including parallel moves, business, and portfolio professions.

The Multi-faceted Nature of Vocation Adaptability

Vocation adaptability envelops different aspects, including position adaptability (work courses of action), ability adaptability (getting new abilities), and job adaptability (moving between various jobs or ventures).

The Changing Idea of Work
The Gig Economy and Outsourcing

The ascent of the gig economy has offered people the chance to function as consultants or self employed entities. This change in work plans offers adaptability yet additionally requires flexibility in dealing with one's profession.

Remote Work and Virtual Joint effort

Mechanical progressions and the Coronavirus pandemic have sped up the reception of remote work. Remote work offers adaptability with regards to area yet requires versatility in correspondence and coordinated effort.

Computerization and the Eventual fate of Occupations

As mechanization and computerized reasoning development, some work jobs might become old. Profession adaptability includes getting ready for these progressions by procuring new abilities and investigating elective vocation ways.

The Significance of Profession Flexibility
Grasping Profession Flexibility

Profession flexibility is the capacity to really deal with one's vocation by changing in accordance with evolving conditions, settling on informed choices, and fostering a proactive mentality.

The Four Elements of Vocation Flexibility

Analyst Imprint L. Savickas recognized four components of vocation flexibility: concern (the inspiration to investigate new open doors), control (the faith in one's capacity to shape their profession), interest (the longing to learn), and certainty (the confidence in one's capacity to effectively adjust).

The Mental Advantages of Profession Versatility

Profession versatility is firmly connected to mental prosperity. People with more elevated levels of vocation flexibility report more noteworthy profession fulfillment, less pressure, and expanded in general life fulfillment.

Techniques for Creating Vocation Versatility

Developing a Development Outlook

A development outlook includes the conviction that capacities and knowledge can be created through exertion and learning. Embracing a development outlook cultivates vocation flexibility by empowering people to see difficulties as any open doors for development.

Long lasting Acquiring and Ability Improvement

Constant learning is fundamental for profession versatility. People ought to put resources into obtaining new abilities and remaining refreshed on industry patterns.

Systems administration and Building Connections

Building areas of strength for an organization gives potential chances to profession versatility. Systems administration can prompt work references, joint efforts, and admittance to coaches who can offer direction during advances.

Genuine Instances of Adaptable Profession Ways

The Portfolio Vocation of Richard Branson

Business person Richard Branson is known for his different endeavors, including Virgin Records, Virgin Atlantic, and Virgin Cosmic. His portfolio vocation mirrors his flexibility and ability to investigate different ventures.

The Progress of Angela Merkel

Angela Merkel, the previous Chancellor of Germany, started her profession as a quantum scientist prior to changing into governmental issues. Her adaptability and flexibility permitted her to succeed in positions of authority and explore complex political scenes.

The Business venture Excursion of Elon Musk

Elon Musk, the business visionary behind organizations like SpaceX and Tesla, has shown vocation versatility by effectively wandering into various enterprises, from space investigation to electric vehicles.

Difficulties in Profession Adaptability

Beating Dread of Progress

The feeling of dread toward change can be a critical hindrance to vocation adaptability. People might oppose leaving their usual ranges of familiarity and seeking after new open doors.

Adjusting Solidness and Adaptability

Offsetting solidness with profession adaptability can challenge. People might wrestle with the requirement for monetary security and the craving to investigate new ways.

Overseeing Vulnerability

Vocation adaptability frequently includes exploring vulnerability. People might have to settle on choices without having an unmistakable guide or dependable results.

Work-Life Reconciliation

The Significance of Balance between serious and fun activities

Accomplishing profession adaptability likewise includes keeping a solid balance between fun and serious activities. People ought to focus on taking care of oneself, family, and individual interests close by their expert interests.

Remote Work and Adaptability

Remote work can offer more prominent work-life combination by permitting people to work from areas that line up with their own lives. Notwithstanding, it additionally demands successful using time productively to forestall burnout.

Strong Workplaces

Associations that advance work-life incorporation and deal adaptable work plans add to representatives' vocation adaptability and prosperity.

The Fate of Work and Profession Adaptability

The Ascent of Mixture Work

The eventual fate of work is supposed to include a crossover model, consolidating remote and in-person work. Vocation adaptability will be fundamental as people adjust to changing work plans.

Abilities for What's to come

In a time of computerization and advanced change, people should consistently obtain and adjust their abilities to stay cutthroat in the gig market.

Business and Advancement

Business venture and development will keep on assuming an essential part in store for work. People with innovative outlooks will be strategically set up to set out their vocation open doors.

5.1 Adapting to Changing Work Environments

The contemporary expert scene is set apart by quick change and advancing workplaces. Globalization, innovative headways, and financial movements have reshaped the manner in which we work. In this investigation of adjusting to changing workplaces, we will dive into the elements of the advanced working environment, the difficulties it presents, techniques for flourishing in the midst of progress, and genuine instances of people and associations that have effectively explored moving workplaces.

The Elements of Present day Workplaces

Figuring out Changing Workplaces

The present workplaces are portrayed by steady advancement. They incorporate remote and half and half work, adaptable timetables, different groups, and advanced coordinated effort devices. Understanding these elements is fundamental for adjusting to change.

The Job of Innovation

Innovation assumes a focal part in changing workplaces. Advanced apparatuses, mechanization, computerized reasoning, and information examination are forming how work is finished and reclassifying position jobs.

Globalization and Variety

Globalization has achieved more prominent variety in work environments, with representatives from various foundations and societies cooperating. Embracing variety and cultivating comprehensive conditions are key parts of adjusting to changing work elements.

The Difficulties of Adjusting to Change

Protection from Change

Human instinct frequently opposes change, prompting opposition among representatives when faced with new workplaces. Beating obstruction is a basic test.

Burnout and Stress

Steady change and expanded requests in current workplaces can prompt burnout and stress. Adjusting to these difficulties requires a proactive way to deal with prosperity.

The Advanced Gap

Not all representatives have equivalent admittance to innovation or the advanced abilities required in contemporary working environments. Spanning the computerized partition is a test associations should address.

Procedures for Adjusting to Changing Workplaces

Developing a Development Outlook

A development outlook includes the conviction that capacities and insight can be created through exertion and learning. Developing this mentality is essential for adjusting to new difficulties and gaining new abilities.

Persistent Learning and Upskilling

In a quickly changing workplace, deep rooted learning is fundamental. People should ceaselessly get new abilities and update existing ones to stay cutthroat.

Viable Correspondence and Coordinated effort

Computerized instruments have made distant cooperation a typical practice. Powerful correspondence, both on the web and disconnected, is crucial for building solid groups and encouraging coordinated effort in changing workplaces.

Genuine Instances of Adjusting to Changing Workplaces
The Change of IBM

IBM, once known fundamentally for equipment and programming, has changed itself into a worldwide innovation benefits and counseling organization. This transformation to changing workplaces required a change in concentration and mastery.

The Remote Work Unrest at Shopify

Shopify, a main internet business stage, embraced remote work and adjusted its strategies to oblige far off representatives. This change permitted them to take advantage of a more extensive ability pool and establish an adaptable workplace.

Adaptable Work at Deloitte

Deloitte, a worldwide counseling firm, embraced adaptable work plans, including "limitless took care of time" and a four-day long week of work in the late spring. This adaptability has further developed representative prosperity and fulfillment.

Encouraging a Versatile Authoritative Culture
The Job of Authority

Pioneers assume a basic part in encouraging a versatile hierarchical culture. They should show others how its done, embrace change, and urge their groups to do likewise.

Building Strength

Associations can assemble versatility by giving assets and backing to workers confronting changes. This incorporates offering preparing programs, psychological well-being backing, and open correspondence channels.

Development and Trial and error

Adjusting to changing workplaces frequently includes trial and error and development. Empowering workers to propose and test groundbreaking thoughts can drive versatility and inventive critical thinking.

Exploring the Change to Half and half Work
The Half breed Work Model

Numerous associations are progressing to crossover work models that join face to face and remote work. Exploring this progress requires clear strategies, innovation framework, and a culture that upholds both in-office and far off representatives.

Difficulties of Crossover Work

Crossover work presents its own arrangement of difficulties, including keeping up with group attachment, tending to value concerns, and guaranteeing powerful correspondence among colleagues in various areas.

Methodologies for Progress

Techniques for progress in a crossover workplace incorporate setting clear assumptions, utilizing innovation to work with coordinated effort, and giving adaptability in work plans.

Embracing Variety and Incorporation

The Significance of Variety and Incorporation

Variety and consideration are fundamental in changing workplaces. Embracing alternate points of view and foundations upgrades inventiveness, advancement, and critical thinking.

Advancing Different Administration

Associations can cultivate variety by advancing different initiative at all levels. This incorporates making mentorship programs, offering racial awareness schooling, and carrying out comprehensive employing rehearses.

Estimating Incorporation Progress

Estimating progress in variety and consideration endeavors is urgent. Associations ought to utilize information and measurements to evaluate the effect of their drives and make essential changes.

The Fate of Work and Flexibility

The Job of Remote Work

Remote work is probably going to stay a huge piece representing things to come of work. Associations should put resources into innovation, online protection, and remote work approaches to help long haul remote or half breed courses of action.

The Gig Economy and Outsourcing

The gig economy, described by transient agreements and independent work, will keep on developing. People might have to adjust to the gig economy by building a different arrangement of clients and abilities.

The Effect of Mechanization and artificial intelligence

As mechanization and man-made reasoning development, certain work jobs might change or become old. Profession flexibility will be vital for people to change into new jobs and ventures.

5.2 Lifelong Learning and Skill Development

In a steadily advancing world set apart by mechanical progressions, financial moves, and changing position showcases, the quest for information and expertise improvement has turned into a deep rooted venture. Deep rooted learning isn't just an individual desire yet an expert need. In this investigation of deep rooted mastering and ability advancement, we will dive into the significance of consistent learning, systems for expertise obtaining, the job of formal and casual training, and genuine instances of people who have embraced long lasting figuring out how to make individual and expert progress.

The Basic of Long lasting Learning

Figuring out Long lasting Learning

Long lasting learning alludes to the progressing, intentional quest for information, abilities, and self-improvement all through one's life. It includes formal training, casual learning, and independent investigation.

The Advancing Idea of Work

Quick mechanical progressions and financial changes have changed the universe of work. Long lasting learning has become fundamental for adjusting to new position jobs, businesses, and vocation ways.

The Crossing point of Individual and Expert Development

Long lasting learning upgrades proficient ability as well as adds to self-improvement and prosperity. It encourages flexibility, versatility, and a feeling of direction.

The Study of Learning

The Brain research of Learning

Mental speculations of learning, like behaviorism, cognitivism, and constructivism, offer experiences into how people obtain information and abilities. Understanding these speculations can illuminate powerful learning techniques.

The Job of Memory and Maintenance

Memory and maintenance are key parts of learning. Methods like separated reiteration, dynamic review, and the utilization of mental aides can upgrade memory and long haul maintenance of data.

Metacognition and Self-Directed Learning

Metacognition, or pondering one's own reasoning, assumes an essential part in viable learning. Self-directed students are proactive in laying out objectives, checking progress, and adjusting their techniques.

Procedures for Deep rooted Mastering and Expertise Improvement

Putting forth Learning Objectives

Putting forth clear and feasible learning objectives is a principal step in long lasting learning. Objectives give guidance, inspiration, and a feeling of direction in the growing experience.

Compelling Using time productively

Overseeing time successfully is fundamental for integrating learning into a bustling timetable. Procedures, for example, time impeding, prioritization, and objective adjusted planning can streamline learning valuable open doors.

Organizing Learning Assets

Admittance to assorted learning assets, including books, courses, webcasts, and online stages, engages people to fit their opportunities for growth to their objectives and interests.

Formal Training and Expertise Improvement

The Worth of Formal Schooling

Formal instruction, like degrees and accreditations, stays important for some professions. It gives organized opportunities for growth, approval of aptitude, and systems administration open doors.

Web based Learning and Advanced Accreditations

The ascent of internet learning stages has made training more available. Computerized certifications, like advanced identifications and microcredentials, empower students to grandstand explicit abilities and accomplishments.

Mixed Learning Models

Mixed learning joins customary study hall guidance with online assets and intelligent exercises. This approach amplifies adaptability while keeping up with the advantages of face to face learning.

Casual Learning and Independent Review

Casual Learning Valuable open doors

Casual learning happens outside organized instructive settings. It incorporates independent review, perusing, going to studios, and taking part in experiential learning.

Independent Review

Independent review permits people to investigate subjects of individual premium and pertinence. It advances independence, interest, and the improvement of decisive reasoning abilities.

Networks of Training

Networks of training are gatherings of people who share a typical interest or calling. Taking part in such networks cultivates cooperative learning and information sharing.

Genuine Instances of Long lasting Learning

The Renaissance of Benjamin Franklin

Benjamin Franklin, a polymath of the eighteenth hundred years, exemplified long lasting learning. Through independent review, he dominated different fields, including science, composing, and tact, contributing altogether to the American Edification.

The Groundbreaking Excursion of Michelle Obama

Previous First Woman Michelle Obama, in the wake of going out, proceeded with her obligation to training and self-improvement. She sent off drives, for example, the "Becoming" book visit and web recording, moving others to embrace deep rooted learning.

The Imaginative Brain of Elon Musk

Elon Musk, known for his endeavors like SpaceX and Tesla, consistently looks for new information and abilities. He has learned advanced science, designing, and man-made reasoning to drive development in his organizations.

Difficulties and Defeating Hindrances

Time Requirements

Occupied timetables and work responsibilities can be obstructions to long lasting learning. Successful using time effectively and prioritization are vital to defeating these difficulties.

Beating Tarrying

Delaying can thwart learning progress. Procedures like breaking undertakings into more modest advances and establishing a favorable learning climate can battle delaying.

Self-Uncertainty and Anxiety toward Disappointment

Self-uncertainty and anxiety toward disappointment can deaden. Developing a development outlook and embracing misfortunes as any open doors for development are fundamental for building flexibility.

The Job of Learning in Proficient Achievement

Expertise Transformation in a Changing Work Scene

The capacity to adjust and acquire new abilities is significant in the present steadily changing position market. Long lasting students are better prepared to explore shifts in work jobs and businesses.

Professional success and Valuable open doors

Ceaseless ability improvement improves profession prospects and opens up new open doors. Deep rooted students frequently have an upper hand in the gig market.

Development and Critical thinking

Long lasting students are bound to add to development and critical thinking in their work environments. They carry new viewpoints and a readiness to investigate groundbreaking thoughts.

The Eventual fate of Deep rooted Learning

Innovative Progressions and Learning

Headways in innovation, for example, augmented reality and man-made brainpower, will alter the manner in which we learn. These advancements will offer vivid and customized opportunities for growth.

The Development of Qualifications

Computerized accreditations, blockchain innovation, and open identifications will keep on reshaping how abilities and accomplishments are perceived and confirmed.

Customized Learning Pathways

Customized learning pathways, custom-made to individual objectives and inclinations, will turn out to be more predominant. Man-made intelligence driven suggestions and versatile learning stages will offer tweaked instructive encounters.

6

Chapter 6

Interpersonal Flexibility

Relational adaptability is a complex idea that assumes a critical part in the elements of human connections. It incorporates the capacity to adjust, comprehend, and discuss really with a different scope of people. In a world set apart by fast friendly and mechanical changes, relational adaptability has arisen as a pivotal expertise for individual and expert achievement. This 3500-word investigation dives into the subtleties of relational adaptability, its significance, advancement, and pragmatic applications in different parts of life.

Figuring out Relational Adaptability

1.1 Definition and Theoretical Structure

Relational adaptability can be characterized as the ability to change one's way of behaving, correspondence style, and profound reactions in different social circumstances. It is established in sympathy, versatility, and successful relational correspondence. At its center, relational adaptability includes perceiving and regarding the one of a kind points of view, requirements, and feelings of others while keeping up with validness.

1.2 The Significance of Relational Adaptability

Relational adaptability is vital in various parts of life, for example,

1.2.1 Individual Connections: In fellowships, relational peculiarities, and heartfelt organizations, being adaptable empowers people to explore clashes, assemble trust, and keep up with sound associations.

1.2.2 Expert Achievement: In the work environment, relational adaptability is vital to successful cooperation, authority, and compromise. It cultivates a positive hierarchical culture and improves vocation development.

1.2.3 Globalization and Variety: In a globalized world, collaborating with individuals from different societies and foundations requests a serious level of adaptability to connect social holes and encourage common comprehension.

1.2.4 Emotional well-being and Prosperity: Relational adaptability is connected to the capacity to understand anyone on a profound level and versatility, the two of which are indispensable for psychological well-being and by and large prosperity.

The Parts of Relational Adaptability

2.1 Capacity to appreciate people at their core

The capacity to understand people on a deeper level, or EQ, is a basic part of relational adaptability. It includes the capacity to perceive, comprehend, and deal with one's own feelings and the feelings of others. High EQ people are better prepared to adjust their reactions and conduct as per the feelings of various circumstances and individuals.

2.2 Sympathy

Compassion is the ability to comprehend and discuss the thoughts of someone else. It is a foundation of relational adaptability, as it empowers people to interface with others on a more profound level, prompting more significant connections and successful correspondence.

2.3 Relational abilities

Viable correspondence is a key part of relational adaptability. It includes verbal as well as non-verbal correspondence. Having the option to convey considerations and feelings plainly, while likewise effectively paying attention to other people, is essential for building compatibility and settling clashes.

2.4 Versatility

Versatility alludes to the capacity to change one's way of behaving and reactions because of evolving conditions. In relational connections, flexibility permits people to explore advancing elements and answer fittingly to new difficulties.

Creating Relational Adaptability

3.1 Mindfulness

Mindfulness is the most vital move towards creating relational adaptability. It includes acquiring one's very own profound comprehension feelings, inclinations, correspondence style, and standards of conduct. This mindfulness gives a strong groundwork to successfully connecting with others.

3.2 Sympathy Preparing

Sympathy can be developed through compassion preparing programs, which assist people with rehearsing point of view taking and foster a more profound comprehension of the feelings and encounters of others.

3.3 Relational abilities Preparing

Relational abilities can be sharpened through different preparation techniques, including studios, pretending activities, and self improvement guides. Successful correspondence includes what is said as well as the way things are said and the way things are gotten.

3.4 Care and Profound Guideline

Care rehearses, like reflection, can assist people with controlling their feelings and answer all the more mindfully in relational connections. This prompts better independent direction and decreased impulsivity.

Relational Adaptability in Various Settings

4.1 Relational Adaptability in Private Connections

4.1.1 Compromise: Adaptability permits people to track down compromises and arrangements during clashes, forestalling relationship crumbling.

4.1.2 Keeping up with Sound Limits: Adjusting individual necessities and the requirements of others requires flexibility and sympathy to guarantee limits are regarded.

4.1.3 Exploring Life Advances: Adaptability assists couples and families with adjusting to significant life altering events, like marriage, being a parent, or migration.

4.2 Relational Adaptability in the Work environment

4.2.1 Powerful Authority: Pioneers who are adaptable in their administration style can persuade different groups and adjust to changing business conditions.

4.2.2 Refereeing: Adaptable people can intercede work environment clashes, cultivating an agreeable workplace.

4.2.3 Group Cooperation: Relational adaptability upgrades collaboration by advancing open correspondence and an eagerness to think about others' thoughts.

4.3 Relational Adaptability in Multifaceted Connections

4.3.1 Multifaceted Correspondence: Understanding and regarding social contrasts considers fruitful communications with individuals from assorted foundations.

4.3.2 Structure Worldwide Connections: Adaptability in multifaceted collaborations encourages global business associations and strategic relations.

The Difficulties of Relational Adaptability

5.1 Over-variation

While flexibility is an important characteristic, over-variation can prompt a deficiency of one's genuine self. People should work out some kind of harmony between acclimating to others' necessities and keeping up with their own personality.

5.2 Profound Fatigue

Continually adjusting to others' feelings can prompt close to home fatigue. It means a lot to rehearse taking care of oneself and defined limits to forestall burnout.

5.3 Protection from Change

A few people might oppose change and display resoluteness in their relational connections. Defeating this opposition frequently requires persistence, compassion, and viable correspondence.

Genuine Instances of Relational Adaptability

6.1 Nelson Mandela: Mandela's capacity to accommodate with his oppressors and lead South Africa through a tranquil progress to a vote based system embodies exceptional relational adaptability.

6.2 Maya Angelou: The prestigious artist and social liberties lobbyist's ability to feel for other people, regardless of her own difficult educational encounters, represents the force of compassion in encouraging significant associations.

6.3 Richard Branson: Branson's adaptable authority style has empowered him to assemble fruitful endeavors in assorted enterprises, from music to space travel.

Relational Adaptability as a Long lasting Excursion

7.1 Nonstop Development

Relational adaptability is definitely not a decent characteristic yet a long lasting excursion. It requires continuous self-reflection, learning, and transformation to changing social elements.

7.2 Beating Difficulties

People might experience deterrents in their quest for more noteworthy relational adaptability. Recognizing and tending to these difficulties is an essential piece of self-improvement.

7.3 Leaving a Heritage

The individuals who develop relational adaptability leave an enduring effect on their connections, associations, and networks by encouraging cooperation, understanding, and positive change.

6.1 Building Strong Relationships

Solid connections are the foundation of a satisfying and significant life. Whether they are with relatives, companions, better halves, or partners, the nature of our associations with others significantly influences our prosperity and in general joy. This 2000-word investigation dives into the specialty of building solid connections, offering bits of knowledge, methodologies, and genuine models that shed light on the multifaceted snare of human association.

The Meaning Areas of strength for of

1.1 Characterizing Solid Connections

Solid connections are described by trust, shared regard, powerful correspondence, and a profound feeling of close to home association. These associations give a feeling of having a place, support, and shared encounters that improve our personal satisfaction.

1.2 The Effect on Prosperity

Solid connections emphatically affect mental and close to home prosperity. They give a cradle against pressure, forlornness, and discouragement, prompting expanded versatility and life fulfillment.

1.3 Kinds of Solid Connections

1.3.1 Familial Bonds: Associations with guardians, kin, and more distant family individuals assume a pivotal part in molding our personalities and emotionally supportive networks.

1.3.2 Fellowships: Dear kinships offer friendship, daily reassurance, and a feeling of having a place.

1.3.3 Heartfelt Associations: Solid close connections give closeness, love, and profound association.

1.3.4 Expert Associations: Building solid expert connections encourages vocation achievement, coordinated effort, and occupation fulfillment.

Underpinnings of Building Solid Connections

2.1 Mindfulness

Mindfulness is the foundation of building solid connections. Figuring out your own qualities, feelings, and correspondence style is critical for shaping significant associations with others.

2.2 Sympathy

Sympathy is the capacity to comprehend and talk about the thoughts of others. It is an essential expertise in building solid connections, as it empowers you to interface with individuals on a more profound level and answer their necessities really.

2.3 Viable Correspondence

Viable correspondence is a basic part serious areas of strength for of. It includes communicating your thoughts obviously as well as effectively tuning in and grasping others' viewpoints.

2.4 Trust and Weakness

Trust is the bedrock of solid connections. Being willing to be open to somebody and entrust them with your feelings and weaknesses cultivates closeness and association.

Procedures for Building Solid Connections

3.1 Contribute Time and Exertion

Building solid connections demands investment and exertion. Put forth a cognizant attempt to support your associations through customary correspondence and getting to know each other.

3.2 Transparent Correspondence

Transparent correspondence is fundamental for settling clashes and keeping up with trust. Energize open exchange, and address issues as they emerge.

3.3 Show Appreciation

Offering thanks and appreciation for your friends and family reinforces your bond. Little tokens of generosity and affirmation can go quite far in building solid connections.

3.4 Be a Decent Audience

Effectively paying attention to others is a strong method for building solid connections. Show that you esteem their contemplations and sentiments by being completely present when they talk.

Building Solid Family Connections

4.1 Parent-Youngster Connections

Building solid parent-kid connections includes offering profound help, defining sound limits, and cultivating open correspondence.

4.2 Kin Bonds

Kin connections can be complicated, yet by effectively dealing with correspondence, settling clashes, and showing affection and backing, solid kin bonds can be manufactured.

4.3 More distant family Associations

Keeping up serious areas of strength for with more distant family individuals requires exertion and a pledge to remaining associated regardless of actual distance or contrasts in points of view.

Building Solid Fellowships

5.1 The Worth of Companionships

Solid fellowships enhance our lives with friendship, daily reassurance, and shared encounters. They can be probably the most persevering and significant connections we have.

5.2 Supporting Fellowships

Sustaining solid companionships includes being dependable, steady, and understanding. Set aside a few minutes for your companions and put resources into their prosperity.

5.3 Managing Struggle

Struggle is unavoidable in any relationship, yet tending to it valuably can reinforce the bond. Move toward clashes with compassion, undivided attention, and an eagerness to track down commonly pleasing arrangements.

Building Solid Heartfelt connections

6.1 The Underpinning of Affection

Solid heartfelt connections are based on affection, trust, and common regard. These connections offer profound closeness, energy, and a deep rooted organization.

6.2 Successful Correspondence in Sentiment

Successful correspondence is particularly basic in close connections. Be open, legitimate, and open to your accomplice to keep areas of strength for a.

6.3 Keeping up with Enthusiasm

Long haul heartfelt connections expect work to keep the enthusiasm alive. This can be accomplished through shared encounters, date evenings, and continuous closeness.

Building Solid Expert Connections

7.1 Systems administration and Joint effort

Solid expert connections are fundamental for vocation achievement. Organizing and teaming up with partners and industry friends can open ways to open doors and headway.

7.2 Compelling Initiative

Compelling initiative includes serious areas of strength for building with colleagues, cultivating a positive work culture, and giving direction and backing.

7.3 Compromise in the Work environment

In the work environment, struggle is unavoidable. Solid expert connections take into consideration the powerful goal of contentions, prompting a more useful and agreeable workplace.

Genuine Instances Areas of strength for of

8.1 Barack and Michelle Obama

The Obamas epitomize serious areas of strength for an organization based on affection, common regard, and a common obligation to public help.

8.2 Oprah Winfrey and Gayle Lord

Oprah and Gayle's long term kinship features the force of profound close to home associations, trust, and steady help.

8.3 Warren Buffett and Charlie Munger

The getting through business association among Buffett and Munger exhibits the significance of trust, shared values, and corresponding abilities in proficient connections.

Conquering Difficulties in Building Solid Connections

9.1 Correspondence Breakdown

Miscommunication and absence of compelling correspondence can strain connections. Tending to correspondence issues through open discourse and undivided attention is significant.

9.2 Trust Issues

Modifying trust after a break can be testing, yet it is conceivable with straightforwardness, consistency, and a pledge to change.

9.3 Adjusting Autonomy

Adjusting autonomy with keeping up serious areas of strength for with is fundamental for self-awareness and solid associations. It's urgent to support your singularity while likewise putting resources into your connections.

6.2 Effective Communication

Powerful correspondence is a central expertise that assumes a urgent part in each part of life. The paste ties connections, the driver of effective coordinated effort, and the groundwork of individual and expert development. In this thorough 2000-word investigation, we will dive profound into the workmanship and study of compelling correspondence, revealing its significance, center standards, obstructions, and pragmatic techniques for dominating this fundamental expertise.

Grasping Powerful Correspondence

1.1 Meaning of Powerful Correspondence

Powerful correspondence alludes to the reasonable, succinct, and significant trade of data between people or gatherings determined to convey considerations, thoughts, sentiments, or expectations precisely.

1.2 The Significance of Viable Correspondence

1.2.1 Structure Connections: Viable correspondence is at the core of solid, significant connections. It encourages trust, compassion, and shared understanding.

1.2.2 Self-awareness: Clear self-articulation and undivided attention are vital to self-awareness, helping people recognize and address their assets and shortcomings.

1.2.3 Expert Achievement: In the work environment, powerful correspondence is fundamental for collaboration, authority, compromise, and professional success.

1.2.4 Worldwide Availability: In an undeniably interconnected world, powerful culturally diverse correspondence is crucial for global relations and worldwide business.

Center Standards of Powerful Correspondence

2.1 Undivided attention

Undivided attention includes concentrating on the speaker, posing explaining inquiries, and giving criticism to guarantee shared understanding. It extends regard and helps construct affinity.

2.2 Clearness and Brevity

Clear and compact correspondence limits false impressions. It includes passing on data straightforwardly and keeping away from language, unclearness, or pointless subtleties.

2.3 Nonverbal Correspondence

Nonverbal signs, like non-verbal communication, looks, and manner of speaking, convey feelings and aims. Monitoring and utilizing these signals really upgrades correspondence.

2.4 Sympathy

Sympathy is the capacity to comprehend and talk about the thoughts of others. It assumes a critical part in building compatibility and exhibiting real consideration in connections.

Boundaries to Compelling Correspondence

3.1 Language and Social Obstructions

Contrasts in language and social standards can frustrate correspondence. Diverse responsiveness and flexibility are fundamental for beating these hindrances.

3.2 Commotion and Interruptions

Outside factors like foundation commotion and interruptions can upset correspondence. Limiting these components and keeping up with center are significant for viable trades.

3.3 Presumptions and Generalizations

Presumptions and generalizations can prompt misinterpretations and miscommunications. It's vital for approach every collaboration with a receptive outlook and without assumptions.

3.4 Profound Obstructions

Compelling feelings, like displeasure, dread, or uneasiness, can obstruct correspondence. Dealing with feelings and utilizing methods like undivided attention can assist with exploring these boundaries.

Procedures for Powerful Correspondence

4.1 Further develop Listening Abilities

Upgrading listening abilities includes giving full consideration, abstaining from intruding, and giving criticism to affirm understanding. This fortifies associations and decreases false impressions.

4.2 Utilize Clear and Succinct Language

Utilizing plain language and keeping away from language or excessively specialized terms guarantees that your message is figured out by a wide crowd.

4.3 Nonverbal Correspondence Authority

Monitoring your own nonverbal prompts and deciphering others' signs precisely conveys and decipher feelings and expectations successfully.

4.4 Practice Sympathy

Compassion can be developed by effectively trying to grasp others' points of view, showing certified interest, and recognizing their feelings.

Viable Correspondence in Private Connections

5.1 Heartfelt Organizations

Compelling correspondence is the underpinning of sound heartfelt connections. It includes communicating adoration, wants, and concerns transparently, and settling clashes with sympathy and understanding.

5.2 Relational intricacies

Clear and empathetic correspondence inside families is indispensable for keeping up major areas of strength for with. It incorporates successful nurturing, settling clashes, and supporting each other's development.

5.3 Fellowships

Solid kinships depend on genuine correspondence and common help. Transparency and compassion assist companions with exploring difficulties and celebrate triumphs together.

Powerful Correspondence in the Work environment

6.1 Group Joint effort

Powerful correspondence among colleagues is fundamental for efficiency and advancement. It includes clear objective setting, open criticism, and cooperative critical thinking.

6.2 Initiative

Powerful pioneers impart their vision, give guidance, and inspire their groups. Solid initiative correspondence cultivates trust, devotion, and achievement.

6.3 Compromise

Struggle is unavoidable in the work environment, yet compelling correspondence can prompt helpful arrangements. Tuning in, looking for shared belief, and compromising are fundamental abilities for compromise.

Powerful Correspondence in Multifaceted Settings

7.1 Social Awareness

In a globalized world, understanding and it is basic to regard different social standards. Diverse correspondence includes adjusting one's correspondence style to connect social holes.

7.2 Language Transformation

While imparting across language obstructions, utilizing clear and straightforward language, motions, and visual guides can improve understanding.

7.3 Worldwide Business

Compelling correspondence in worldwide business includes thinking about social subtleties, language capability, and adjusting exchange styles to cultivate useful organizations.

Genuine Instances of Compelling Correspondence

8.1 Nelson Mandela

Mandela's capacity to connect racial partitions and lead South Africa to compromise is a demonstration of the force of successful correspondence in governmental issues and strategy.

8.2 Maya Angelou

The eminent artist and social equality extremist's capacity to pass general human encounters on through her words epitomizes the effect of compelling correspondence in writing and activism.

8.3 Steve Occupations

Occupations' ability for enamoring crowds with his item dispatches shows the way that powerful correspondence can drive business achievement and brand dedication.

Difficulties and Traps in Powerful Correspondence

9.1 Distortion

Indeed, even with all that expectations, misinterpretations can happen because of social contrasts, tone, or setting. Tending to misconceptions with persistence and compassion is vital.

9.2 Overcommunication

While clearness is fundamental, inordinate correspondence can overpower and befuddle. Finding some kind of harmony between giving fundamental data and staying away from data over-burden is vital.

9.3 Evasion of Troublesome Discussions

Keeping away from troublesome discussions can prompt unsettled clashes and stressed connections. Figuring out how to move toward testing conversations with sympathy and emphaticness is fundamental.

Chapter 7

**Health and Wellness
Through Flexibility**

Wellbeing and health are complex ideas that envelop physical, mental, and close to home prosperity. While numerous perspectives add to a sound way of life, adaptability is many times a neglected at this point significant part. In this complete 3500-word guide, we will investigate the significance of adaptability in accomplishing ideal well-being and health. We will dig into the physical, mental, and profound components of adaptability, examine its advantages, give functional tips to improving adaptability, and deal experiences into its job in different parts of life.

Grasping Adaptability

1.1 What Is Adaptability?

Adaptability alludes to the capacity of the muscles, ligaments, and tendons to stretch and travel through their full scope of movement. It is a vital part of actual wellness and a fundamental part of generally prosperity.

1.2 The Components of Adaptability

Adaptability includes a few aspects:

1.2.1 Static Adaptability: The capacity to extend a muscle and stand firm on it in a drawn out situation.

1.2.2 Unique Adaptability: The ability to move the slightest bit and joint through a scope of movement with control.

1.2.3 Dynamic Adaptability: The capacity to utilize one's muscle solidarity to keep a joint's scope of movement.

1.2.4 Inactive Adaptability: The ability to utilize outer power (e.g., an accomplice or a prop) to broaden a joint's scope of movement.

The Significance of Adaptability in Actual Wellbeing

2.1 Adaptability and Joint Wellbeing

Keeping up with joint adaptability is fundamental for forestalling wounds and decreasing the gamble of conditions like joint pain. Adaptable joints are less inclined to strain and harm.

2.2 Adaptability and Solid Wellbeing

Adaptable muscles are more averse to turn out to be tight and inclined to injury. Integrating adaptability practices into your routine can lighten muscle strain and distress.

2.3 Adaptability and Stance

Great stance depends on adjusted muscle tone and adaptability. Keeping up with adaptability can assist with forestalling stance related issues like back agony and spinal bend.

2.4 Adaptability and Actual Execution

Adaptability is imperative for competitors and people took part in proactive tasks. It further develops dexterity, equilibrium, and in general athletic execution.

Mental Adaptability and Mental Wellbeing

3.1 Mental Adaptability Characterized

Mental adaptability is the ability to adjust to new data, thoughts, and circumstances. A mental expertise assumes a critical part in critical thinking and direction.

3.2 Mental Advantages of Mental Adaptability

3.2.1 Improved Critical thinking: People serious areas of strength for with adaptability can move toward issues from numerous points, prompting innovative and viable arrangements.

3.2.2 Pressure Decrease: Being intellectually adaptable permits people to really adjust to stressors and adapt to difficulties more.

3.2.3 Better Learning: Adaptable reasoning upgrades the capacity to retain new data and obtain new abilities.

3.2.4 Better Independent direction: Mental adaptability empowers people to consider various choices and settle on all around informed choices.

Close to home Adaptability and Mental Prosperity

4.1 Close to home Adaptability Characterized

Close to home adaptability alludes to the ability to adjust to changing feelings and answer them in a sound and useful way. It includes figuring out, directing, and communicating feelings actually.

4.2 Close to home Advantages of Profound Adaptability

4.2.1 Close to home Flexibility: Sincerely adaptable people are better prepared to quickly return from misfortunes and difficulty.

4.2.2 More grounded Connections: Understanding and dealing with feelings cultivates better relational connections.

4.2.3 Diminished Uneasiness and Misery: Profound adaptability can lessen the gamble of tension and gloom by advancing close to home guideline.

4.2.4 Expanded Life Fulfillment: An adaptable way to deal with feelings can prompt more noteworthy by and large prosperity and life fulfillment.

The Actual Advantages of Adaptability Preparing

5.1 Better Scope of Movement

Standard adaptability preparing expands joint and muscle adaptability, upgrading your capacity to move unreservedly and serenely.

5.2 Decreased Muscle Pressure and Touchiness

Extending practices discharge muscle pressure and decrease post-practice touchiness, advancing unwinding and recuperation.

5.3 Injury Counteraction

Adaptable muscles and joints are less vulnerable to injury, as they can all the more likely endure abrupt developments and strains.

5.4 Better Stance

Adaptability practices assist with keeping up with great stance, decreasing the gamble of back torment and other stance related issues.

The Psychological and Close to home Advantages of Adaptability Preparing

6.1 Improved Mental Flexibility

Taking part in adaptability preparing cultivates mental versatility, permitting you to move toward difficulties and changes with a more open and adjusted outlook.

6.2 Pressure Decrease

Normal adaptability practices advance unwinding and stress decrease by delivering strain and quieting the sensory system.

6.3 Profound Guideline

Adaptability preparing can work on close to home guideline by advancing care and mindfulness, empowering you to successfully deal with your feelings more.

Down to earth Ways to further develop Adaptability

7.1 Integrate Extending into Your Everyday practice

Incorporate both static and dynamic stretches in your activity routine. Extending ought to be done routinely, in a perfect world when active work.

7.2 Yoga and Pilates

Yoga and Pilates are incredible practices that underscore adaptability, balance, and mental mindfulness. Think about coordinating these disciplines into your wellness schedule.

7.3 Spotlight on Relaxing

Profound, careful breathing during extending activities can upgrade the unwinding reaction and further develop adaptability.

7.4 Continuous Movement

Begin gradually and progressively increment the force and term of your extending schedules. Try not to drive your body into outrageous positions.

Adaptability in Day to day existence

8.1 Adaptability in Critical thinking

Applying mental adaptability to everyday difficulties can prompt more viable arrangements and diminished pressure.

8.2 Adaptability in Profound Reactions

Being genuinely adaptable permits you to answer different circumstances with poise, advancing mental prosperity.

8.3 Adaptability in Connections

Adaptability in correspondence and compromise can further develop connections by advancing comprehension and participation.

Adaptability in Proficient Life

9.1 Flexibility in the Working environment

Flexibility is a significant expertise in proficient settings. Representatives who can acclimate to changing conditions and embrace new difficulties are profoundly esteemed.

9.2 Viable Correspondence

Adaptability in correspondence advances coordinated effort, decreases mistaken assumptions, and improves collaboration in the working environment.

9.3 Profession Development

Embracing adaptability in your vocation, like securing new abilities and adjusting to industry changes, can prompt proficient headway.

7.1 Mind-Body Connection

The brain body association is an idea that has captivated rationalists, researchers, and medical care experts for a really long time. It places that our psychological and profound states are personally entwined with our actual prosperity. This many-sided connection between the brain and the body has significant ramifications for our wellbeing, influencing everything from our insusceptible framework to our capacity to oversee ongoing sicknesses. In this thorough investigation, we will dive into the brain body association, its authentic roots, the logical proof supporting it, and its down to earth suggestions for medical services and day to day existence.

Verifiable Points of view

The idea of the psyche body association has antiquated roots, with early human advancements perceiving the connection among mental and actual wellbeing. In old Greece, scholars like Hippocrates and Plato considered the impact of the brain on substantial wellbeing. Hippocrates, frequently called the "Father of Medication," accepted that psychological and close to home variables assumed a huge part in the improvement of sicknesses.

Eastern customs, like Ayurveda and Customary Chinese Medication, additionally stressed the significance of harmony among mental and actual parts of wellbeing. These antiquated frameworks of medication perceived that profound uneven characters could prompt actual sicknesses and looked to reestablish amicability in both the psyche and the body.

René Descartes, a conspicuous savant of the seventeenth hundred years, presented the possibility of dualism, which recommended that the psyche and body were discrete

elements. This thought made a split between the domains of mental and actual wellbeing, making way for later conversations on the brain body association.

Logical Approval

The logical investigation of the psyche body association picked up speed in the twentieth 100 years, as scientists revealed proof supporting that our psychological and close to home states could impact our actual wellbeing.

Stress and the Safe Framework: One of the most all around concentrated on parts of the brain body association is the effect of weight on the invulnerable framework. Persistent pressure has been connected to debilitated safe capability, making people more powerless to contaminations and infections. This association between mental pressure and actual wellbeing is currently generally acknowledged in the clinical local area.

Self-influenced consequence: A self-influenced consequence is a striking illustration of the brain's capacity to impact actual results. At the point when people accept they are getting a valuable treatment, regardless of whether it is a fake treatment (an idle substance), they frequently experience genuine upgrades in their condition. This peculiarity highlights the strong job of the psyche in recuperating.

Mind-Body Mediations: Practices like contemplation, yoga, and care have acquired notoriety as of late for their beneficial outcomes on both mental and actual wellbeing. Studies have demonstrated the way that these psyche body mediations can diminish pressure, lower circulatory strain, and work on generally prosperity.

Psychoneuroimmunology: This interdisciplinary field of examination analyzes the collaborations between the anxious, endocrine, and invulnerable frameworks. Psychoneuroimmunology has given significant experiences into how mental elements, like feelings and stress, can adjust insusceptible reactions and effect wellbeing results.

Mind-Body Medication: Brain body medication is an arising field that coordinates mental, close to home, and social elements into clinical practice. It perceives that addressing the brain body association can prompt better understanding results and worked on by and large wellbeing.

Commonsense Ramifications

Comprehensive Medical services: Medical services suppliers are progressively embracing an all encompassing methodology that considers the psyche and body as

interconnected. This approach perceives that tending to mental and close to home prosperity is fundamental for generally speaking wellbeing.

Stress The board: Perceiving the unfavorable impacts of persistent weight on actual wellbeing, stress the executives strategies, for example, care contemplation and unwinding practices are being incorporated into medical services and health programs.

Reciprocal Treatments: Integral and elective treatments that attention on the psyche body association, like needle therapy, biofeedback, and fragrant healing, are acquiring notoriety as assistants to ordinary clinical medicines.

Way of life Changes: Way of life changes, including ordinary activity, a decent eating regimen, and sufficient rest, are pivotal for keeping a solid brain body harmony.

Emotional well-being: The psyche body association highlights the significance of tending to psychological well-being issues instantly. Untreated emotional wellness conditions can negatively affect actual wellbeing.

Patient Strengthening: Patients are turning out to be more engaged to play a functioning job in their medical care by understanding the psyche body association and taking on rehearses that advance both mental and actual prosperity.

Mind-Body Association and Constant Sicknesses

Irritation and Immune system Problems: Persistent pressure and gloomy feelings can add to foundational irritation, which assumes a vital part in the turn of events and movement of immune system sicknesses like rheumatoid joint pain and lupus.

Cardiovascular Wellbeing: Mental pressure and close to home variables can influence cardiovascular wellbeing by raising pulse, expanding the gamble of coronary illness, and adding to the improvement of atherosclerosis.

Torment The executives: Psyche body methods, like mental social treatment and care, have been demonstrated to be successful in overseeing ongoing agony conditions, offering an option in contrast to conventional torment drugs.

Diabetes Control: Stress and uneasiness can influence glucose levels in people with diabetes. Overseeing pressure through unwinding strategies can help improve glycemic control.

Malignant growth and Mental States: While the psyche body association can't forestall disease, it can impact malignant growth results. Positive mental states have been related with better adapting, worked on personal satisfaction, and, surprisingly, improved endurance rates among malignant growth patients.

Mind-Body Association in Psychological well-being

Despondency and Tension: Ongoing pressure and profound misery are connected to the advancement of temperament issues like sorrow and uneasiness. These circumstances can, thus, influence actual well-being by expanding the gamble of ongoing sicknesses.

Psychosomatic Ailment: Psychosomatic sickness alludes to actual side effects or conditions that are basically caused or exacerbated by mental elements. Models incorporate strain cerebral pains, crabby gut disorder (IBS), and fibromyalgia.

Synapses and Feelings: The cerebrum's synapses, like serotonin and dopamine, assume a significant part in controlling feelings. Disturbances in these synapse frameworks can prompt temperament problems and have actual appearances.

Care Based Treatments: Care based treatments, similar to Care Based Pressure Decrease (MBSR) and Care Based Mental Treatment (MBCT), have demonstrated successful in diminishing side effects of sadness and nervousness by advancing mindfulness and close to home guideline.

Injury and PTSD: Injury and post-horrendous pressure problem (PTSD) can make enduring actual impacts, remembering changes for the mind's construction and capability. Tending to the psyche body association is fundamental in injury recuperation.

Mind-Body Association in Maturing

Mental Wellbeing: There is developing proof that way of life factors, including mental excitement, social commitment, and profound prosperity, can impact mental wellbeing in more established grownups. Positive mental states might assist with deferring the beginning old enough related mental deterioration.

Constant Torment in Seniors: Numerous more established grown-ups experience ongoing agony conditions, and the psyche body association is urgent in overseeing torment and working on personal satisfaction in this populace.

Dejection and Segregation: Forlornness and social confinement can antagonistically affect both mental and actual wellbeing in seniors. Keeping up serious areas of strength for with associations is fundamental for by and large prosperity.

Care and Maturing: Care practices can be especially useful for more established grown-ups, assisting them with adapting to the difficulties of maturing, lessen pressure, and improve their general personal satisfaction.

Functional Systems for Upgrading the Brain Body Association

Care Contemplation: Care reflection includes focusing on the current second without judgment. Normal practice can diminish pressure, upgrade profound guideline, and work on in general prosperity.

Work out: Actual work has indisputably factual advantages for both mental and actual wellbeing. It discharges endorphins, lessens pressure, and further develops state of mind.

Unwinding Methods: Strategies like moderate muscle unwinding, profound breathing activities, and directed symbolism can advance unwinding and lessen pressure.

Solid Eating regimen: A decent eating routine wealthy in supplements can uphold both mental and actual prosperity. Supplement thick food varieties give the structure blocks important to mind capability and generally wellbeing.

Social Associations: Keeping up areas of strength for with associations and looking for help from companions and friends and family is essential for profound prosperity.

Profound Articulation: It's fundamental for express and cycle feelings as opposed to suppressing them. Journaling, conversing with a specialist, or taking part in imaginative outlets can help.

7.2 Flexible Approaches to Fitness and Nutrition

In the present unique world, unbending wellness and nourishment plans may not be useful or supportable all the time. Our lives are loaded up with flighty timetables, steadily evolving needs, and one of a kind individual necessities. To address these difficulties, adaptable ways to deal with wellness and sustenance have acquired fame. These methodologies perceive that one size doesn't fit all, and they adjust to individual objectives, inclinations, and conditions. In this complete aide, we will investigate the

idea of adaptable wellness and nourishment, look at its advantages, and give useful procedures to integrate adaptability into your wellbeing process.

Grasping Adaptability in Wellness and Nourishment

Adaptability in wellness and sustenance alludes to the capacity to adjust and alter your wellbeing rehearses in view of your singular necessities and evolving conditions. It includes perceiving that life is erratic, and inflexible plans may not be maintainable 100% of the time. Adaptable methodologies focus on long haul prosperity over momentary flawlessness.

Key Components of Adaptable Wellness and Sustenance:

Flexibility: Being available to changing your wellness and sustenance systems in light of evolving conditions, for example, a bustling plan for getting work done, travel, or unforeseen occasions.

Individualization: Fitting your wellness and sustenance plans to your one of a kind objectives, inclinations, and prerequisites, instead of sticking to a one-size-fits-all methodology.

Supportability: Zeroing in on rehearses that you can keep up with over the long haul, as opposed to outrageous or prohibitive strategies that are challenging to maintain.

Balance: Taking a stab at a fair methodology that incorporates different food varieties and exercise modalities to advance both physical and mental prosperity.

Careful Eating: Focusing on yearning and completion signs, as well as the profound parts of eating, to cultivate a solid relationship with food.

Advantages of Adaptable Wellness and Nourishment

Supportability: Adaptable methodologies are bound to be maintainable over the long haul. They permit you to adjust to life's promising and less promising times without wrecking your advancement.

Individualization: By fitting your wellness and sustenance practices to your one of a kind necessities, you can accomplish your particular objectives all the more successfully and with more noteworthy fulfillment.

Mental Prosperity: Adaptable methodologies focus on mental prosperity by lessening the pressure and tension frequently connected with inflexible eating fewer carbs and practice regimens.

Further developed Relationship with Food: Embracing adaptability in sustenance energizes a better relationship with food, diminishing the probability of cluttered dietary patterns.

Assortment: Adaptable wellness and sustenance advance assortment in your schedules, which can forestall weariness and levels while improving physical and mental commitment.

Versatile to Life Changes: Life is loaded with changes, and an adaptable methodology permits you to change your wellbeing practices to oblige new conditions, like pregnancy, injury, or changing work responsibilities.

Down to earth Techniques for Adaptable Wellness

Practice Assortment: Integrate an assortment of activity modalities into your daily schedule, for example, strength preparing, cardiovascular exercises, adaptability activities, and exercises you truly appreciate. This forestalls weariness and diminishes the gamble of abuse wounds.

Stand by listening to Your Body: Focus on your body's signs. On the off chance that you're feeling exhausted, it's OK to take a rest day or participate in delicate development like yoga or extending.

Change Your Timetable: Life can be unusual. On the off chance that you can't come to the rec center or your typical activity class, track down elective ways of moving, for example, a speedy home exercise or a stroll during your mid-day break.

Put forth Reasonable Objectives: Lay out objectives that are testing yet feasible. Try not to put forth excessively aggressive objectives that might prompt burnout or injury.

Focus on Consistency: Consistency is vital to long haul progress. Center around little, manageable changes that you can keep up with over the long haul.

Mingle and Remain Dynamic: Join associating with actual work by taking part in bunch wellness classes, sporting games, or open air undertakings with companions or family.

Reasonable Systems for Adaptable Sustenance

Natural Eating: Practice instinctive eating by paying attention to your body's craving and completion signs. Eat when you're eager and stop when you're fulfilled, instead of sticking to severe feast times or carbohydrate contents.

Adjusted Diet: Embrace a decent eating routine that incorporates different supplement rich food sources. Keep away from outrageous or prohibitive weight control plans that dispense with whole nutritional categories.

Dinner Arranging: Plan your feasts and bites in light of your timetable and wholesome necessities. Get ready compact snacks for occupied days to try not to go with undesirable food decisions when you're in a hurry.

Careful Eating: Dial back and appreciate your dinners. Stay away from interruptions like telephones or TV while eating to partake in the tactile experience of food completely.

Infrequent Treats: Permit yourself incidental treats or extravagances without responsibility. Partaking in your #1 food sources with some restraint can assist with forestalling sensations of hardship.

Adaptability with Dietary Limitations: In the event that you have dietary limitations or sensitivities, investigate elective fixings and recipes to adjust your #1 dishes.

Adaptability in Extraordinary Conditions

Travel: Travel frequently upsets schedule. Focus on development by investigating your objective by walking, and pick better choices while eating out. Pack nutritious snacks for the excursion.

Pregnancy: Pregnancy requires changes in both wellness and sustenance. Talk with medical care experts to make a protected and adaptable arrangement that obliges your evolving needs.

Injury or Sickness: Wounds and diseases may briefly restrict your active work. Center around restoration and look for direction from medical services suppliers on safe activities.

Stress and Profound Eating: Stress can prompt close to home eating. Practice pressure the board methods like contemplation, profound breathing, or participating in loosening up exercises.

Evolving Objectives: As your objectives advance, be available to changing your wellness and sustenance plans. Whether you're moving from weight reduction to upkeep or progressing to another athletic undertaking, adjust your techniques as needs be.

Tracking down Help and Responsibility

Proficient Direction: Consider talking with wellness mentors, enlisted dietitians, or nutritionists who spend significant time in adaptable methodologies. They can give customized direction custom-made to your necessities and objectives.

Online People group: Join online discussions or virtual entertainment bunches that advance adaptable wellness and sustenance. These people group can offer help, motivation, and viable counsel.

Responsibility Accomplices: Cooperate with a companion or relative who shares your obligation to adaptable wellbeing rehearses. Having a responsibility accomplice can keep you roused and on target.

Following and Diaries: Keep a wellness or sustenance diary to screen your advancement and consider how adaptable methodologies are helping your general prosperity.

Chapter 8

Overcoming Challenges

Challenges are an intrinsic piece of life. They come in different structures, from individual snags like self-uncertainty and affliction to outer troubles like monetary emergencies and worldwide pandemics. While confronting difficulties can be overwhelming, they are additionally open doors for development, strength, and self-improvement. In this far reaching investigation, we will dive into the idea of difficulties, the brain science behind beating them, and pragmatic techniques to explore and overcome life's impediments.

Figuring out Difficulties

What Are Difficulties?

Challenges are circumstances or deterrents that require exertion, transformation, and critical thinking to survive. They can be outer, for example, business related troubles, or inside, such as overseeing pressure or self-question. Difficulties can differ generally in extension, force, and span, however they are widespread encounters that touch each part of human existence.

The Idea of Difficulties

Certainty: Difficulties are an essential piece of the human experience. Nobody is safe to them, and they emerge in different areas of life, including profession, connections, wellbeing, and self-awareness.

Subjectivity: What one individual sees as a test may not be no different for another. Individual encounters, points of view, and conditions shape how difficulties are characterized and drawn nearer.

Amazing open doors for Development: Difficulties, when explored actually, can prompt self-awareness, versatility, and the advancement of significant fundamental abilities. They can be groundbreaking encounters that push people past their usual ranges of familiarity.

Transitory Nature: Difficulties are not super durable. While some might endure for broadened periods, they are not difficult, and they frequently contain important illustrations.

The Brain science of Difficulties

The Pressure Reaction: Difficulties trigger the body's pressure reaction, including the arrival of cortisol and adrenaline. Understanding what stress means for the body and brain is fundamental for overseeing it really.

Mentality: A development outlook, rather than a decent attitude, can essentially influence how people see and tackle difficulties. Embracing the conviction that one can learn, adjust, and work on despite misfortune encourages flexibility.

Survival techniques: Individuals utilize different ways of dealing with hardship or stress to manage difficulties. A few techniques are versatile, such as looking for help or critical thinking, while others are maladaptive, similar to evasion or refusal.

Procedures for Defeating Difficulties

1. Creating Flexibility

Flexibility is the capacity to quickly return from affliction and keep up with mental prosperity. An expertise can be developed through the accompanying methodologies:

1. **Building Serious areas of strength for a Framework**
   Family, companions, tutors, and care groups can offer profound help and useful direction during testing times.
2. **Creating The capacity to appreciate people at their core**
   Understanding and dealing with one's own feelings and relating to others can improve strength notwithstanding relational difficulties.
3. **Rehearsing Self-Sympathy**
   Being benevolent and understanding toward oneself, particularly during difficulties, can support flexibility and keep self-analysis from subverting progress.
4. **Developing Versatility**

Embracing change and vulnerability as any open doors for development can assist people with adjusting all the more successfully to startling difficulties.

2. Objective Setting and Arranging

1. **Brilliant Objectives**
   Setting Explicit, Quantifiable, Reachable, Important, and Time-bound (Savvy) objectives gives a reasonable system to advance and accomplishment.
2. **Separate Complex Objectives**
   Separating bigger objectives into more modest, reasonable errands makes them not so much overpowering but rather more attainable.
3. **Adaptability in Arranging**

While arranging is essential, it's similarly critical to stay open to changes and elective
ways when difficulties emerge.

3. Critical thinking and Navigation

1. **Distinguish the Issue**
   Characterize the test obviously and unbiasedly, recognizing its underlying drivers and likely outcomes.
2. **Create Arrangements**
   Conceptualize numerous arrangements, taking into account both customary and whimsical methodologies.
3. **Assess and Pick**
   Evaluate the advantages and disadvantages of every arrangement, taking into account achievability, assets, and expected results. Select the most proper strategy.
4. **Execution and Assessment**

Set the picked arrangement in motion and assess its adequacy. Be ready to change the arrangement if essential.

4. Embracing Disappointment and Gaining from Mishaps

1. **Destigmatize Disappointment**
   Perceive that disappointment is a characteristic piece of the growing experience and doesn't characterize one's worth or capacities.
2. **Remove Illustrations**
   In the wake of confronting difficulties, ponder the experience to distinguish significant illustrations, bits of knowledge, and regions for development.
3. **Strength Even with Disappointment**

Use misfortunes as any open doors to construct strength, flexibility, and assurance.

5. Stress The executives

1. **Care and Reflection**
   Care practices can assist people with remaining grounded and lessen pressure by zeroing in on the current second.

2. **Actual work**

Ordinary activity discharges endorphins, which can lighten pressure and work on generally prosperity.

3. **Unwinding Procedures**

Profound breathing activities, moderate muscle unwinding, and directed symbolism can assist with overseeing pressure.

4. **Look for Proficient Assistance**

In the event that pressure becomes overpowering or ongoing, think about looking for help from a specialist or guide.

6. Using time productively and Prioritization

1. **Time Usage Instruments**

Use apparatuses like plans for the day, schedules, and time-following applications to really oversee assignments and cutoff times.

2. **Focus on Assignments**

Recognize assignments that are generally significant and time-touchy, zeroing in on finishing them first.

3. **Put down Stopping points**

Lay out clear limits to safeguard individual time and forestall burnout.

7. Looking for Help and Assets

1. **Proficient Assistance**

For challenges connected with psychological well-being, vocation, or self-improvement, looking for direction from experts like specialists, profession guides, or holistic mentors can give important bits of knowledge and techniques.

2. **Encouraging groups of people**

Joining support gatherings, whether face to face or on the web, can give a feeling of having a place and admittance to shared encounters and arrangements.

8. Building Self-Viability

1. **Authority Encounters**
   Accomplishing little triumphs fabricates certainty and a faith in one's capacity to conquer difficulties.

2. **Vicarious Learning**
   Noticing other people who have confronted and vanquished comparative difficulties can rouse and illuminate one's own methodology.

3. **Verbal Influence**
   Consolation and positive criticism from others can support self-viability.

4. **Close to home States**

Overseeing tension and self-uncertainty through unwinding procedures and positive self-talk can improve self-viability.

Applying Methodologies to Genuine Difficulties

1. **Vocation Difficulties**
   Tending to work related difficulties, for example, working environment clashes, employment misfortune, or profession changes, requires a mix of strength, critical thinking, and systems administration abilities.

2. **Relationship Difficulties**
   Conquering relationship challenges, whether in companionships, relational peculiarities, or heartfelt associations, frequently includes powerful correspondence, compassion, and compromise.

3. **Wellbeing and Health Difficulties**
   Overseeing wellbeing challenges, for example, ongoing diseases, emotional well-being issues, or way of life changes, requires

a comprehensive methodology that incorporates physical, profound, and social prosperity.

4. **Monetary Difficulties**

Exploring monetary difficulties, including obligation, planning, or unforeseen costs, includes monetary education, arranging, and asset the board.

5. **Self-improvement Difficulties**

Challenges connected with self-awareness, like self-disclosure, personal growth, or seeking after interests, benefit from self-sympathy, objective setting, and flexibility.

Genuine Accounts of Beating Difficulties

1. **The Strength of Nelson Mandela**
Nelson Mandela's excursion from detainee to president is a demonstration of strength, pardoning, and assurance even with political mistreatment.

2. **Oprah Winfrey's Victory Over Difficulty**
Oprah Winfrey's troublesome youth and early profession battles didn't hinder her from turning into a news big shot and giver.

3. **Stephen Selling's Victory Over Actual Constraints**
Famous physicist Stephen Peddling's noteworthy work went on in spite of a finding of ALS (Lou Gehrig's illness) and serious actual handicaps.

4. **J.K. Rowling's Way to Scholarly Achievement**

Creator J.K. Rowling's excursion from neediness and dismissal to the making of the worldwide darling Harry Potter series embodies versatility and innovative steadiness.

8.1 Resilience in Adversity

Versatility in affliction is the ability to astound of people to quickly return from life's most troublesome conditions, rising up out of difficulty more grounded, savvier, and stronger than previously. Even with difficulties like individual misfortune, injury, monetary mishaps, or wellbeing emergencies, versatility enables people to make due as well as flourish. This extensive investigation digs into the idea of strength, the elements that impact it, and reasonable methodologies to develop and tackle flexibility while confronting affliction.

Figuring out Flexibility

What Is Versatility?

Versatility is a diverse idea including mental, profound, and pragmatic credits that empower people to adjust emphatically to misfortune. It's anything but a proper characteristic but instead a unique quality that can be created and fortified over the long run. Strength outfits people with the psychological and profound backbone to explore life's difficulties without surrendering to surrender.

Key Parts of Strength

Profound Guideline: Versatile people are capable at dealing with their feelings, which permits them to adapt to pressure, nervousness, and trouble actually.

Positive Mentality: Keeping a confident and hopeful viewpoint, even despite misfortune, is a sign of versatility. This positive outlook supports a singular's capacity to persevere through difficulty.

Versatility: Strong people are adaptable and versatile, embracing change as a chance for development instead of a danger.

Social Help: Having a vigorous emotionally supportive network of companions, family, or a local area can give a basic cradle during testing times.

Critical thinking Abilities: The capacity to distinguish issues, create arrangements, and make proactive strides is indispensable to strength.

Self-Empathy: Versatile people practice self-sympathy, offering themselves generosity and understanding during troublesome minutes.

The Significance of Flexibility

Improved Adapting: Strong people have the apparatuses to adapt actually to difficulty, lessening the gamble of creating constant pressure or psychological wellness issues.

Worked on Prosperity: Flexibility adds to in general prosperity, cultivating an uplifting perspective, more noteworthy life fulfillment, and expanded joy.

Self-awareness: Difficulty can be an impetus for self-awareness, and tough people frequently rise up out of difficulties with freshly discovered qualities and bits of knowledge.

Social Association: Versatility encourages more grounded social securities, as people who display flexibility are in many cases seen as strong and motivational figures inside their networks.

Elements Impacting Versatility

1. **Strong Connections**

   Having an organization of strong connections, including companions, family, coaches, or specialists, gives profound food during testing times.

2. **Fearlessness and Self-Adequacy**

   Having confidence in one's capacities and ability to conquer misfortune is a foundation of versatility.

3. **Close to home Guideline**

   The capacity to oversee and explore feelings in a solid way is essential for strength. Methods like care and the ability to understand anyone on a profound level can be important in such manner.

4. **Critical thinking Abilities**

   Compelling critical thinking abilities empower people to make a move and recover a feeling of control while confronting difficulty.

5. **Positive Survival techniques**

   Taking part in certain survival methods, like activity, imaginative outlets, or unwinding procedures, can support versatility.

6. **Versatility**

   The ability to adjust to change and vulnerability without becoming overpowered is a sign of versatility.

7. **Feeling of Direction**

   An unmistakable feeling of direction or importance in life can give inspiration and course during troublesome times.

8. **Idealism**

   Keeping a confident and hopeful standpoint assists people persevere through misfortune with more noteworthy flexibility.

9. **Gaining from Affliction**

Seeing affliction as a chance for development and learning can improve strength.

Procedures for Developing Strength

Versatility is an expertise that can be created and sharpened over the course of life. Here are functional systems to develop and outfit flexibility notwithstanding misfortune:

1. **Construct and Sustain Steady Connections**

   Put resources into significant associations with loved ones. These associations can

   offer significant profound help during testing times.

2. **Practice Taking care of oneself**

   Focus on taking care of oneself exercises like activity, contemplation, satisfactory rest, and a decent eating routine to keep up with physical and profound prosperity.

3. **Foster Profound Mindfulness**

   Develop the ability to appreciate anyone on a profound level by expanding mindfulness and perceiving close to home examples. This can support dealing with feelings during affliction.

4. **Put forth Reasonable Objectives**

   Separate difficulties into more modest, sensible objectives.

Accomplishing these achievements can support self-assurance and strength.

5. **Embrace Change**

Foster a versatile outlook that perspectives change as a chance for development as opposed to a danger. Tolerating that change is a steady piece of life can diminish opposition and cultivate versatility.

6. **Look for Proficient Assistance**

While confronting huge difficulty, think about looking for direction from a specialist or instructor. Proficient help can offer significant experiences and ways of dealing with stress.

7. **Keep up with Viewpoint**

While experiencing affliction, step back and think about the master plan. This more extensive viewpoint can assist with decreasing the effect of prompt difficulties.

8. **Develop Self-Empathy**

Indulge yourself with the very graciousness and understanding that you would offer a companion confronting misfortune. Self-sympathy cultivates versatility by lessening self-analysis.

9. **Develop Positive thinking**

Cultivate a confident standpoint by zeroing in on certain parts of circumstances, tracking down silver linings, and recognizing past triumphs in beating difficulty.

10. **Gain from Misfortune**

Think about difficulties and mishaps to separate illustrations and experiences. Utilize these encounters as any open doors for self-improvement.

11. **Foster Critical thinking Abilities**

Upgrade your capacity to distinguish issues, produce arrangements, and make a move. Critical thinking abilities are basic to flexibility.

Genuine Instances of Flexibility

1. **Malala Yousafzai - Instruction Supporter and Nobel Laureate**
   In spite of being designated by the Taliban for upholding young ladies' schooling, Malala Yousafzai has turned into a worldwide image of strength and a promoter for instructive privileges.
2. **Viktor Frankl - Holocaust Survivor and Psychotherapist**
   Viktor Frankl's encounters in Auschwitz death camp drove him to create logotherapy and state "Man's Quest for Significance," underlining the significance of tracking down reason and importance notwithstanding languishing.
3. **Maya Angelou - Famous Artist and Creator**
   Maya Angelou's strong diary "I Know Why the Confined Bird Sings" relates her encounters of life as a youngster injury and bigotry, displaying her flexibility and ability to motivate others.
4. **Elon Musk - Business visionary and Trend-setter**

Elon Musk confronted various business mishaps and individual difficulties, yet he proceeds to advance and drive forward with historic endeavors like SpaceX and Tesla.

8.2 Embracing Failure for Growth

Disappointment is much of the time seen as a difficulty, a barrier on the way to progress. Notwithstanding, a change in perspective is in progress, empowering people to see disappointment as a significant and unavoidable piece of the excursion. Embracing disappointment for development is a groundbreaking methodology that assists people with bouncing back from mishaps as well as pushes them toward more significant levels of progress, versatility, and self-improvement. In this far reaching investigation, we will

dive into the idea of embracing disappointment, the mental elements at play, and viable systems for transforming disappointments into venturing stones toward development and accomplishment.

Grasping Disappointment
What Is Disappointment?

Disappointment is comprehensively characterized as the absence of progress or the non-accomplishment of an ideal objective or result. It can appear in different parts of life, including individual connections, schooling, vocation, and imaginative pursuits. Disappointment is emotional and can go from minor misfortunes to additional huge frustrations.

The Idea of Disappointment

Certainty: Disappointment is an inborn part of life. Nobody is resistant to it, and, surprisingly, the most achieved people have encountered their reasonable part of difficulties.

Subjectivity: What one individual sees as disappointment may not be no different for another. Individual encounters, objectives, and assumptions shape how disappointment is characterized.

Learning A valuable open door: Disappointment presents a chance for learning and development. It is a fruitful ground for acquiring bits of knowledge, building flexibility, and refining one's methodology.

Strength Developer: Confronting and beating disappointment can upgrade one's flexibility, the capacity to quickly return from misfortune more grounded than previously.

The Apprehension about Disappointment

The feeling of dread toward disappointment is a typical mental boundary that can keep people from facing challenges, seeking after their objectives, and understanding their true capacity. It can appear as uneasiness, compulsiveness, or tarrying. Defeating the feeling of dread toward disappointment is a basic move toward embracing it as an impetus for development.

The Brain science of Embracing Disappointment

The Development Mentality

The development mentality, an idea promoted by clinician Song Dweck, is fundamental to embracing disappointment for development. People with a development mentality

accept that their capacities and insight can be created through exertion and learning. This outlook cultivates strength and an eagerness to embrace provokes and misfortunes as any open doors to get to the next level.

Mental Flexibility

Embracing disappointment is firmly connected to mental flexibility, the capacity to adjust emphatically to affliction and stress. Strong people view disappointment as an impermanent misfortune and are bound to return with recharged assurance. Strength can be developed through different systems and practices.

Self-Empathy

Self-empathy includes treating oneself with graciousness, understanding, and absolution, especially despite disappointment. It lessens self-analysis and hairsplitting, making it simpler to see disappointment as a piece of the growing experience.

Beating Dread and Uneasiness

Apprehension about disappointment can incapacitate people, keeping them from facing challenges or chasing after their objectives. Methods like openness treatment, care, and reexamining can help people go up against and deal with their feeling of dread toward disappointment.

Embracing Weakness

Recognizing weakness is a fundamental piece of embracing disappointment. Weakness includes being available to the chance of disappointment and uneasiness, which can prompt genuine and significant development encounters.

Methodologies for Embracing Disappointment for Development

1. **Shift Your Viewpoint**

   Rethink disappointment as a characteristic piece of the educational experience. View it as a valuable chance to accumulate data, refine your methodology, and develop.

2. **Set Reasonable Assumptions**

   Lay out reasonable objectives and assumptions. Try not to set unthinkably elevated expectations that improve the probability of seen disappointment.

3. **Practice Self-Empathy**

   Be thoughtful and understanding toward yourself when you experience disappointment. Stay away from self-analysis and negative self-talk.

4. **Develop a Development Mentality**

   Cultivate a conviction that capacities and insight can be created through exertion and learning. Embrace moves as any open doors to develop.

5. **Gain from Disappointment**

   Consider your disappointments to remove illustrations, bits of knowledge, and regions for development. Utilize these encounters to illuminate your future activities.

6. **Go ahead with Potentially dangerous courses of action**

   Get out of your usual range of familiarity and go ahead with potentially dangerous courses of action. Perceive that not all dangers will prompt achievement, however every one offers an opportunity to learn and develop.

7. **Look for Criticism**

   Request criticism from tutors, companions, or specialists. Helpful criticism can give significant experiences and guide your development process.

8. **Develop Flexibility**

   Construct mental strength by rehearsing pressure the executives procedures, keeping an uplifting perspective, and looking for help when required.

9. **Embrace Weakness**

Recognize and acknowledge weakness as a piece of life. Embracing weakness takes into account valid encounters and significant development.

Genuine Instances of Embracing Disappointment

1. **Thomas Edison - The Designer of the Light**
   Thomas Edison is frequently celebrated for his various bombed endeavors to make the electric light. He broadly said, "I have not fizzled. I've quite recently found 10,000 different ways that won't work." His determination and ability to embrace disappointment at last prompted perhaps of the main development ever.

2. **J.K. Rowling - The Creator of Harry Potter**
   Prior to making huge progress with the Harry Potter series, J.K. Rowling confronted various dismissals from distributers. Her excursion from misfortune to scholarly fame is a demonstration of embracing disappointment for development.

3. **Oprah Winfrey - The News Head honcho**
   Oprah Winfrey's wild childhood and early profession misfortunes didn't prevent her from turning into a news investor, giver, and persuasive figure. She has transparently shared her encounters of conquering difficulty.

4. **Michael Jordan - The Ball Legend**

Michael Jordan, generally viewed as one of the best ball players ever, broadly missed a huge number of shots and lost many games during his vocation. He attributes his prosperity to his capacity to embrace disappointment and use it as inspiration.